I0438945

Analysis and Simulation of Water-Level, Specific Conductance, and Total Phosphorus Dynamics of the Loxahatchee National Wildlife Refuge, Florida, 1995–2006

By Paul A. Conrads and Edwin A. Roehl, Jr.

Prepared as part of the U.S. Geological Survey Greater Everglades Priority Ecosystem Science

Scientific Investigations Report 2010–5244

U.S. Department of the Interior
U.S. Geological Survey

U.S. Department of the Interior
KEN SALAZAR, Secretary

U.S. Geological Survey
Marcia K. McNutt, Director

U.S. Geological Survey, Reston, Virginia: 2010

For more information on the USGS—the Federal source for science about the Earth, its natural and living resources, natural hazards, and the environment, visit *http://www.usgs.gov* or call 1-888-ASK-USGS

For an overview of USGS information products, including maps, imagery, and publications, visit *http://www.usgs.gov/pubprod*

To order this and other USGS information products, visit *http://store.usgs.gov*

Suggested citation:
Conrads, P.A., and Roehl, E.A., Jr., 2010, Analysis and simulation of water-level, specific conductance, and total phosphorus dynamics of the Loxahatchee National Wildlife Refuge, Florida, 1995–2006: U.S. Geological Survey Scientific Investigations Report 2010–5244, 64 p.

Contents

Figures

Tables

Conversion Factors and Datums

Multiply	By	To obtain
Length		
inch	2.54	centimeter (cm)
foot (ft)	0.3048	meter (m)
mile (mi)	1.609	kilometer (km)
Area		
acre	4,047	square meter (m^2)
acre	0.4047	hectare (ha)
square mile (mi^2)	259.0	hectare (ha)
square mile (mi^2)	2.590	square kilometer (km^2)
Flow rate		
cubic foot per second (ft^3/s)	0.02832	cubic meter per second (m^3/s)

Temperature in degrees Celsius (°C) may be converted to degrees Fahrenheit (°F) as follows:

$$°F = (1.8 \times °C) + 32$$

Temperature in degrees Fahrenheit (°F) may be converted to degrees Celsius (°C) as follows:

$$°C = (°F - 32) / 1.8$$

Vertical coordinate information is referenced to the National Geodetic Vertical Datum of 1929 (NGVD 29).

Horizontal coordinate information is referenced to the North American Datum of 1983 (NAD 83).

Elevation, as used in this report, refers to distance above the vertical datum.

Acronyms and Abbreviations Used in this Report

AI	artificial intelligence
ANN	artificial neural network
BEP	back error propagation
CERP	Comprehensive Everglades Restoration Plan
CRADA	Cooperative Research and Development Agreement
DSS	decision support system
EVPA	Everglades Protection Area
GH	gage height
GUI	graphical user interface
LOX	water-quality sampling sites in the EVPA monitoring network
LOXANN DSS	Loxahatchee Artificial Neural Network Decision Support System
ME	mean error
MS	Microsoft
MSE	mean square error
NWIS	National Water Information System
OLS	ordinary least squares
PME	percent model error
Q	flow
Refuge	Arthur R. Marshall Loxahatchee Wildlife Refuge
RMSE	root mean square error
R^2	coefficient of determination
SC	specific conductance
SFWMD	South Florida Water Management District
SIANN	Spatially Interpolating Artificial Neural Network
SSE	sum of square error
STA	Stormwater Treatment Area
TP	total phosphorus
USACE	U.S. Army Corps of Engineers
USFWS	U.S. Fish and Wildlife Service
USGS	U.S. Geological Survey
UTM	Universal Transverse Mercator
WL	water level
XYZ	District transect water quality monitoring network
3DVis	three-dimensional visualization

Analysis and Simulation of Water-Level, Specific Conductance, and Total Phosphorus Dynamics of the Loxahatchee National Wildlife Refuge, Florida, 1995–2006

By Paul A. Conrads[1] and Edwin A. Roehl, Jr.[2]

Abstract

The Arthur R. Marshall Loxahatchee Wildlife Refuge (Refuge) was established in 1951 through a license agreement between the South Florida Water Management District and the U.S. Fish and Wildlife Service (USFWS) as part of the Migratory Bird Conservation Act. Under the license agreement, the State of Florida owns the land of the Refuge and the USFWS manages the land. Fifty-seven miles of levees and borrow canals surround the Refuge. Water in the canals surrounding the marsh is controlled by inflows and outflows through control structures. The transport of canal water with higher specific conductance and nutrient concentrations to the interior marsh has the potential to alter critical ecosystem functions of the marsh.

Data-mining techniques were applied to 12 years (1995–2006) of historical data to systematically synthesize and analyze the dataset to enhance the understanding of the hydrology and water quality of the Refuge. From the analysis, empirical models, including artificial neural network (ANN) models, were developed to answer critical questions related to the relative effects of controlled releases, precipitation, and meteorological forcing on water levels, specific conductance, and phosphorous concentrations of the interior marsh. Data mining is a powerful tool for converting large databases into information to solve complex problems resulting from large numbers of explanatory variables or poorly understood process physics. For the application of the linear regression and ANN models to the Refuge, data-mining methods were applied to maximize the information content in the raw data. Signal processing techniques used in the data analysis and model development included signal decomposition, digital filtering, time derivatives, time delays, and running averages. Inputs to the empirical models included time series, or signals, of inflows and outflows from the control structures, precipitation, and evapotranspiration. For a complex hydrologic system like the Refuge, the statistical accuracy of the models and predictive capability were good. The water-level models have coefficient of determination (R^2) values ranging from 0.90 to 0.98. The R^2 for the specific conductance model is 0.82, and the R^2 for the total phosphorus model is 0.51. The accuracy of the models was attributable to the quantity and quality of the available data.

To make the models directly available to all stakeholders, an easy-to-use decision support system (DSS) called the Loxahatchee Artificial Neural Network Model (LOXANN) DSS was developed as a spreadsheet application that integrates the historical database, linear regression and ANN models, model controls, streaming graphics, and model output. The LOXANN DSS allows Refuge managers and other users to easily execute the water level, specific conductance, and phosphorous models to evaluate various water-resource management scenarios. The user is able to choose from three options in setting the control-structure flows: as a percentage of historical flow, as a constant flow, or as a user-defined hydrograph. Output from the LOXANN DSS includes tabular time series of predictions of the measured data and predictions of the user-specified conditions. A three-dimensional visualization routine also was developed that displays longitudinal specific conductance conditions.

Two scenarios were simulated with the LOXANN DSS. One scenario increased the historical flows at four control structures by 40 percent. The second scenario used a user-defined hydrograph to set the outflow from the Refuge to the weekly average inflow to the Refuge delayed by 2 days. Both scenarios decreased the potential of canal water intruding into the marsh by decreasing the slope of the water level between the canals and the marsh.

---

[1] U.S. Geological Survey, South Carolina Water Science Center, Columbia, SC.

[2] Advanced Data Mining, LLC, Greenville, SC.

Introduction

The Arthur R. Marshall Loxahatchee National Wildlife Refuge (Refuge) is the last of the soft-water ecological systems in the Everglades. "Soft-water" systems have low calcium or magnesium ions as compared to "hard water" systems with higher concentrations of calcium or magnesium. Historically, the ecosystem was driven by precipitation inputs that were low in specific conductance and nutrients (fig. 1). Fifty-seven miles of levees and borrow canals surround the Refuge and the water in the canals have higher concentrations of calcium and magnesium ion compared to the Refuge water. The banks of the canal by the interior marsh are not continuous, with openings of various sizes where marsh water exchanges with water from the canals. With controlled flow releases into and out of the canals that surround the Refuge, the transport of water from the canals with higher specific conductance (an indirect measurement of ionic concentration such as calcium and magnesium) and nutrient concentration has the potential to alter critical ecosystem functions of the interior marsh (fig. 2). With potential alteration of flow patterns to accommodate the restoration of the Everglades, the Refuge could be affected not only by changes in the timing and frequency of flows releases into the canals but by the quality of the water that inundates the Refuge.

Hydrologic and water-quality data have been collected in the Refuge for many years. Data characterizing the hydrology of the system—inflows, outflows, precipitation, and water levels—have been collected since the 1950s. Data characterizing the water quality of the system, including specific conductance and total phosphorus, have been collected since the late 1970s. New technologies in environmental monitoring have made it cost effective to acquire tremendous amounts of hydrologic and water-quality data. The monitoring networks supported by the Comprehensive Everglades Restoration Plan (CERP) record tremendous amounts of data each day, and the database incorporates millions of measurements that describe the environmental response of the system to changing conditions. Often these active and historical databases are underinterpreted and underutilized. Although these data are a valuable resource for understanding environmental systems, a thorough synthesis and analysis of the data may be lacking. New methodologies are available to systematically synthesize and analyze the dataset to answer critical questions related to the relative effects of controlled releases, precipitation, groundwater interaction, and meteorological forcing on water level, specific conductance, and phosphorous concentration to enhance the understanding of the hydrology and water quality of the interior marsh of the Refuge.

The U.S. Geological Survey (USGS) entered into a Cooperative Research and Development Agreement (CRADA) with Advanced Data Mining International in 2002 to collaborate on applying data mining and artificial neural network (ANN) models to water-resources investigations. The emerging field of data mining addresses the issue of extracting information from large databases (Weiss and Indurkhya, 1998). Data mining is a powerful tool for converting large databases into information for use in solving problems that are otherwise imponderable because of the large numbers of explanatory variables or poorly understood process physics. Data-mining methods come from different technical fields—such as signal processing, statistics, artificial intelligence, and advanced visualization—and include methods for maximizing the information content of data, determining which variables have the strongest correlations to the problems of interest, and developing models that predict future outcomes. This knowledge encompasses both understanding of cause and effect relations and predicting the consequences of alternative actions. Data mining is used extensively in financial services, banking, advertising, manufacturing, and e-commerce to classify the behaviors of organizations and individuals and to predict future outcomes.

Purpose and Scope

This report presents the results of an investigation that analyzed water level (gage height), specific conductance, and total phosphorus dynamics in the Refuge caused by changing inflows, outflows, precipitation, and evapotranspiration conditions. In this report, the terms water level and gage height are used interchangeably. This report documents the development of the Loxahatchee Artificial Neural Network Decision Support System (LOXANN DSS), including examples of applying the LOXANN DSS to the Refuge to evaluate the intrusion of canal water into the marsh.

An important part of the USGS mission is to provide scientific information for the effective water-resources management of the Nation. To assess the quantity and quality of the Nation's surface-water, the USGS collects hydrologic and water-quality data from rivers, lakes, and estuaries by using standardized methods and maintains the data from these stations in a national database. Often these databases are underutilized and under-interpreted for addressing contemporary hydrologic issues. The techniques presented in this report demonstrate how valuable information can be extracted from existing disparate databases to assist local, State, and Federal agencies understand and manage complex hydrologic systems. The application of data-mining techniques, including ANN models, to the Refuge demonstrates how empirical models of complex hydrologic systems can be developed, disparate databases and models can be integrated, and study results can easily be disseminated to meet the needs of a broad range of end users.

FLORIDA GEOLOGICAL SURVEY BULLETIN TWENTY-FIVE—FIGURE 71

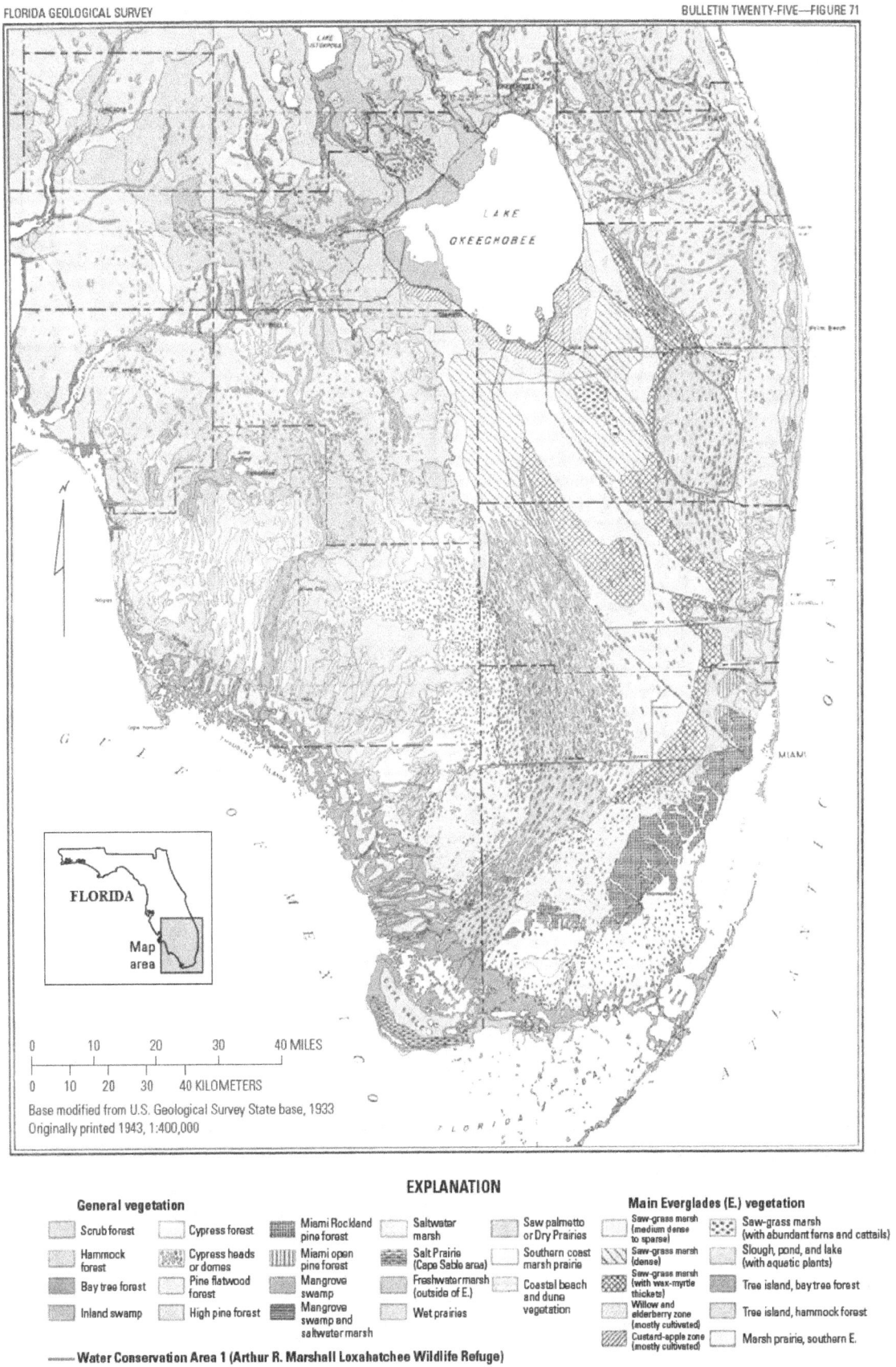

EXPLANATION

Figure 1. Vegetation map of southern Florida circa 1943 (modified from Davis, 1943). The Arthur R. Marshall Loxahatchee Wildlife Refuge vegetation type is characterized as slough, pond, and lake (with aquatic plants).

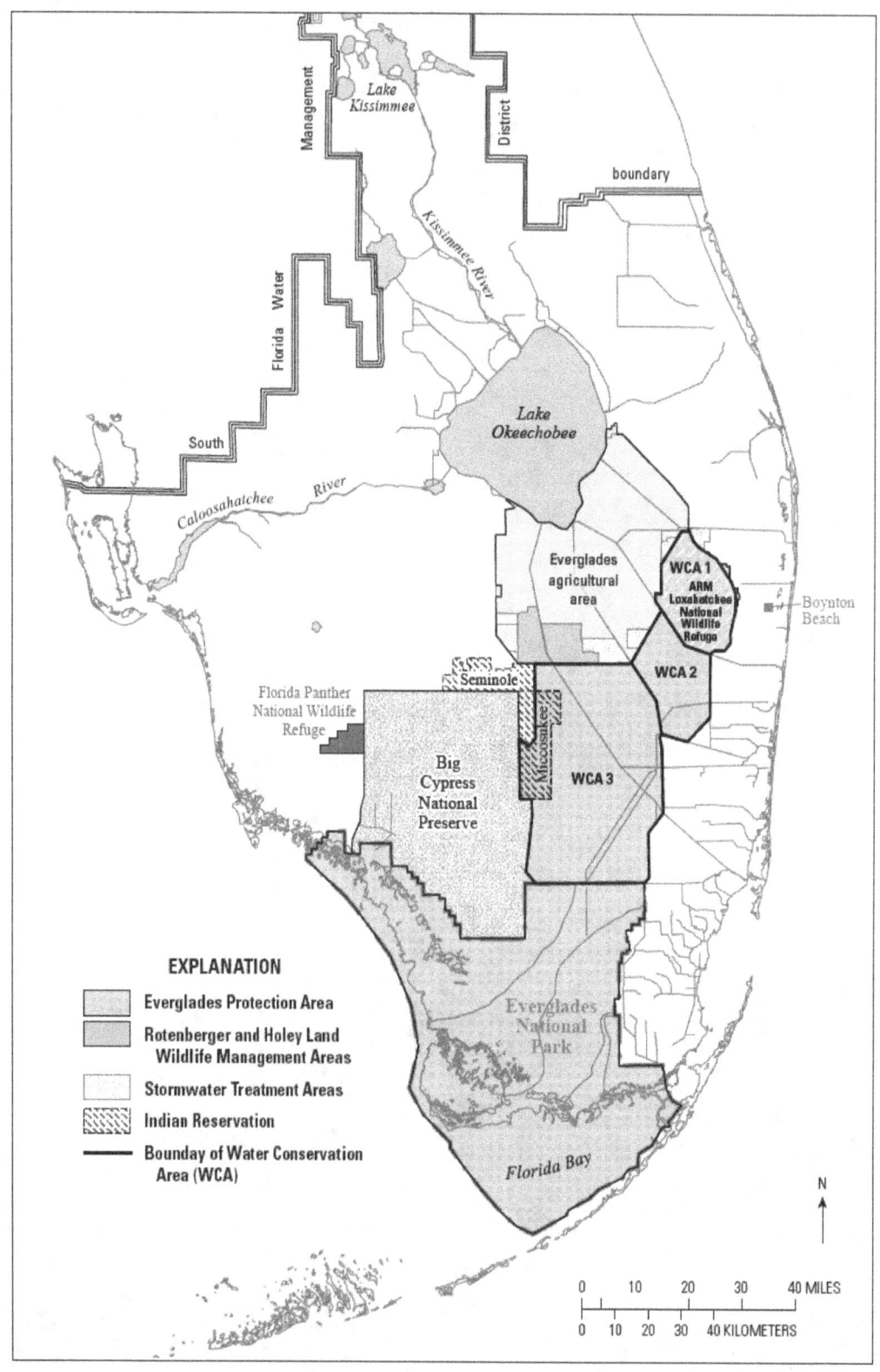

Figure 2. The Arthur R. Marshall (ARM) Loxahatchee National Wildlife Refuge and the Water Conservation Areas of the Everglades, Florida (modified from U.S. Fish and Wildlife Service, 2000).

Description of the Study Area

Historically, the area of the present day Refuge was part of an uninterrupted wetland that extended from Lake Okeechobee and flowed to the southwestern tip of Florida (Richardson and others, 1990; fig. 1). Beginning in the mid 1800s, drainage activities began to convert the wetlands for agriculture and urban development. In the 1940s, the U.S. Army Corps of Engineers (USACE) constructed Water Conservation Areas 1, 2, and 3 to regulate water for the increasing population and agricultural needs of South Florida through a series of levees and canals (fig. 2). In general, the Water Conservation Areas store water during the wet season and supply water during the dry season.

The 143,238-acre Loxahatchee National Wildlife Refuge (Water Conservation Area 1) was established in 1951 through a license agreement between the South Florida Water Management District (SFWMD) and the U.S. Fish and Wildlife Service (USFWS) as part of the Migratory Bird Conservation Act (U.S. Fish and Wildlife Service, 2000). Under the license agreement, the State of Florida owns the land of the Refuge and the USFWS manages the land. Water in the Refuge is controlled by inflows and outflows through control structures to the 57 miles of canals that surround the Refuge (fig. 3). The eastern boundary of the refuge is the L-40 canal, and the western boundary of the Refuge is formed by the L-7 canal to the northwest and the L-39 canal (also known as the Hillsboro Canal) to the southwest. Land use surrounding the Refuge varies with the Everglades Agricultural Area to the northwest, urban areas to the east, and the Water Conservation Areas of the Everglades to the south and southwest. In 1986, the name of the Refuge was changed to A.R.M. Loxahatchee National Wildlife Refuge to honor the local conservationist Arthur R. Marshall.

Although the Refuge is regulated hydrologically, it is considered a "unique remnant which still functions as a northern refuge for species of the Everglades ecosystem" (Richardson and others, 1990). The limestone bottom of the freshwater marsh of the Refuge is overlain with peat as much as 12 feet thick, and the approximate land-elevation gradient is 5 feet from north to south (U.S. Fish and Wildlife Service, 2007a). Richardson and others (1990) describes the interior of the Refuge as a "complex mosaic of wetland communities that grade from wetter areas such as sloughs and wet prairies, to sawgrass, brush, and finally tree islands occurring at the drier end of the scale (fig. 4)." The plant community of the Refuge developed under nutrient-poor conditions and was maintained with a continuation of low nutrient concentrations (Walker, 1995). A change in the nutrient-poor conditions of the marsh may adversely affect the plant community structure.

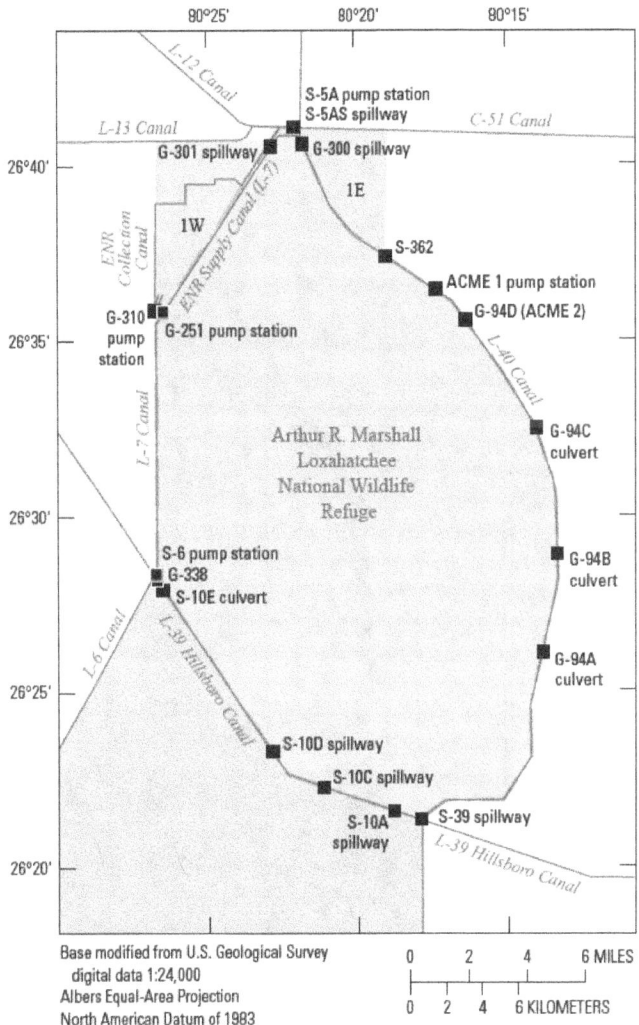

Base modified from U.S. Geological Survey digital data 1:24,000
Albers Equal-Area Projection
North American Datum of 1983

EXPLANATION

Water Conservaton Area

   1

   2

1W   **Stormwater-treatment area and identifier**

L-6 Canal   **Canal and identifier**

G-301 spillway ■ **Control structure and identifier**

Figure 3. Water conservation areas, stormwater treatment areas, and boundary canals near the Arthur R. Marshall Loxahatchee National Wildlife Refuge, Florida.

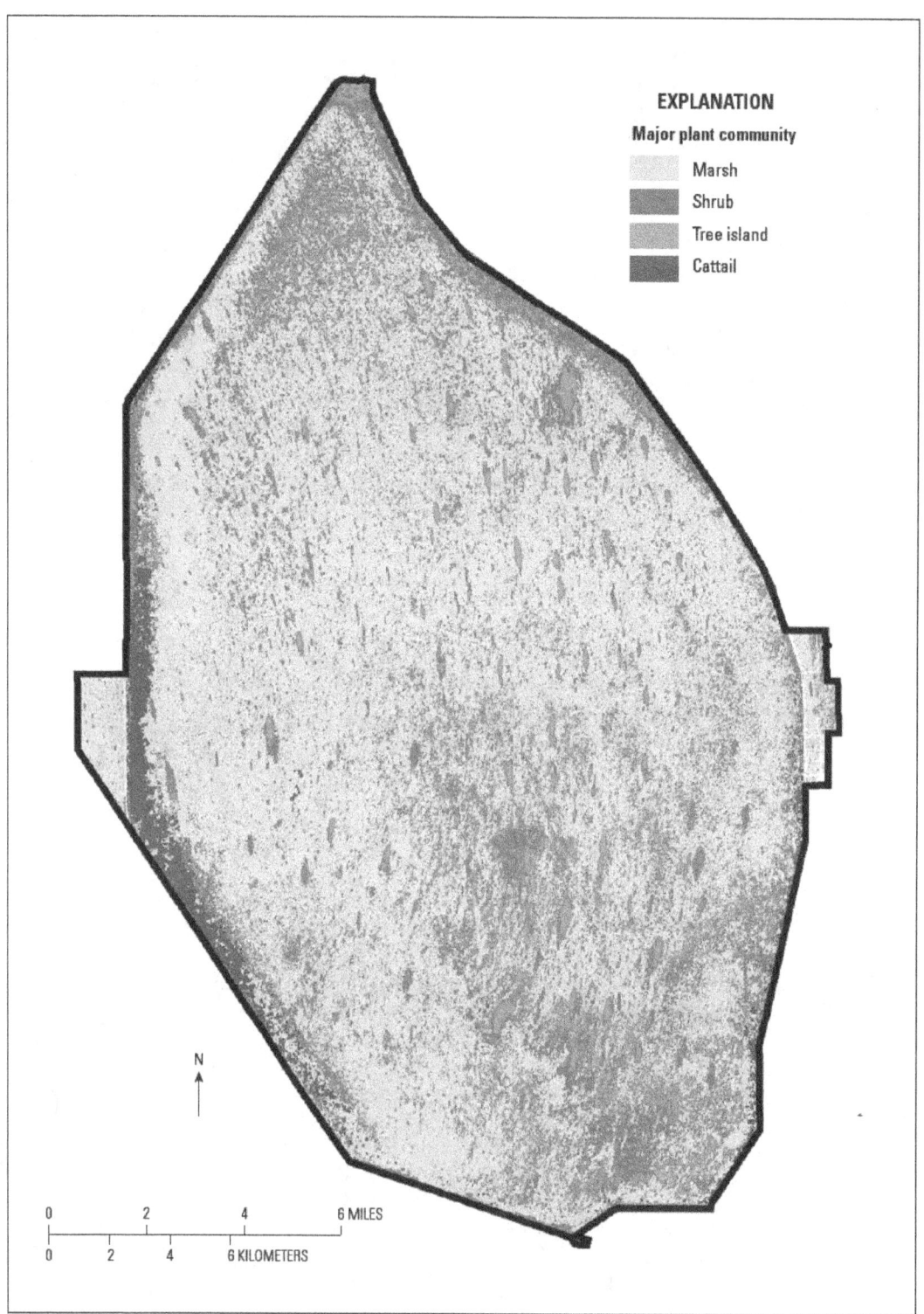

Figure 4. The four major plant communities of the Arthur R Marshall Loxahatchee National Wildlife Refuge, Florida (modified from Richardson and others, 1990).

Historically, the major sources of water to the area of the Refuge were precipitation and sheetflow from the wetlands with a low nutrient load to the system. With the development of agricultural, suburban, and urban areas, and the channelization of flow to and around the Refuge, the nutrient load, especially phosphorus, increased substantially (greater than 100 parts per billion [ppb]; Walker, 1995). In 1994, the Florida legislature passed the Everglades Forever Act with one of its goals being the reduction of phosphorus concentrations in the Everglades to less than 50 ppb with the ultimate goal of reducing concentrations to less than 10 ppb. The Act provided funding for the construction of stormwater treatment areas (STAs) to reduce the phosphorus load to the Water Conservation Areas and Everglades National Park (fig. 2). Stormwater treatment areas 1E and 1W were constructed to reduce excess nutrient loads to the Refuge (fig. 3). The STAs are large (greater than 6,000 acres) constructed wetlands with a series of cells with varying hydraulic characteristics, aquatic plants, and periphyton mats that uptake phosphorus from inflow from the Everglades Agricultural Area before releasing the water to the Refuge.

Currently, the major sources of water to the Refuge are rainfall (56 percent), the S-5A pump station (40 percent), and the ACME-1 and ACME-2 pump stations (4 percent) (U.S. Fish and Wildlife Service, 2007a). Of all the water pumped into the Refuge, approximately 91 percent is drained from the Everglades Agricultural Area, and 9 percent is from agricultural and urban developed lands located east of the Refuge (U.S. Fish and Wildlife Service, 2007a). The water level in the canals is managed through a cooperative agreement among the USACE, SFWMD, and USFWS, referred to as a Water Regulation Schedule (U.S. Fish and Wildlife Service, 2007a; fig. 5), to meet the needs of the Refuge and its downstream uses. The current schedule was implemented in 1995 and designed to

(1) maintain the health of the Refuge vegetation types by flooding all wetlands during the summer and fall; (2) enhance feeding opportunities for waterfowl and wading birds by lowering water levels in the spring so that water is concentrated in sloughs and shallow ponds during nesting season; (3) maintain water storage capacity in the Refuge during the hurricane season; (4) store water for irrigating nearby cropland during the fall, winter, and early spring; and (5) prevent saltwater intrusion into the Biscayne aquifer by storing water for release into coastal canal systems during the fall, winter, and spring (U.S. Fish and Wildlife Service, 2000).

Previous Studies

Numerous ecological and hydrologic studies have been conducted to support the management of the Refuge and the resulting changes of the water-level and water-quality dynamics of the canals and marshes of the Refuge. Many of the plant ecology studies have focused on the characterization of the plant communities and how these communities respond to changing soil pore-water quantity and quality. Many of the hydrodynamic and water-quality modeling studies have focused on developing simulation models to estimate water level and water quality in the canals and marshes. These models have been used to evaluate various hydrologic scenarios and their effect on plant community dynamics, water-regulation schedules, and alternative water management. A thorough summary of hydrodynamic and water-quality models applied to the Everglades in general and the Refuge in particular can be found in Arceneaux and others (2007). Additional information on model development funded by the Refuge can be found in the annual reports of their Enhanced Monitoring and Modeling Program (U.S. Fish and Wildlife Service, 2007a, 2007b, and 2009).

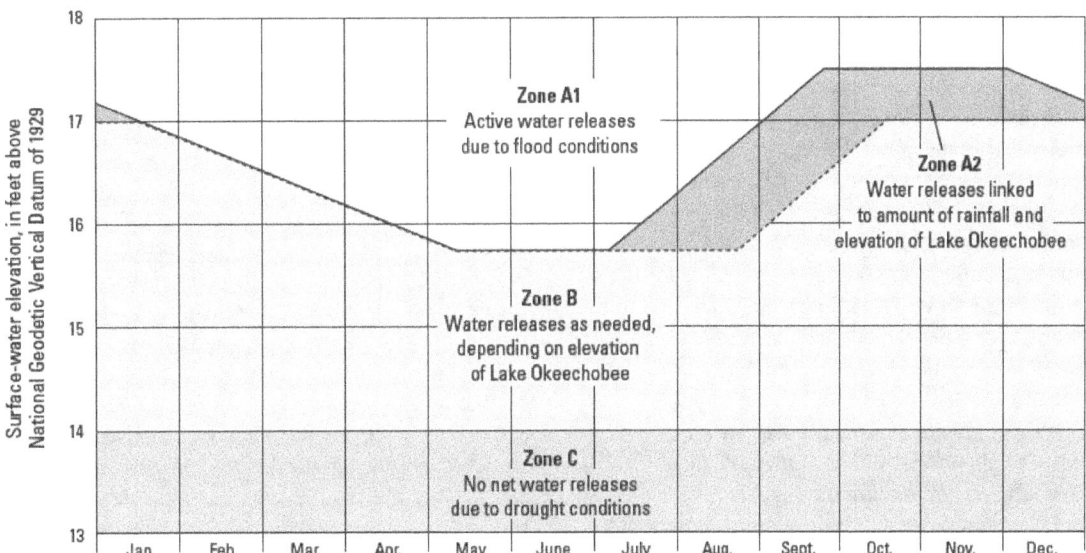

Figure 5. Water regulation schedule for Water Conservation Area 1, Arthur R. Marshall Loxaxatchee National Wildlife Refuge (modified from U.S. Fish and Wildlife Service, 2000; see figure 2 for location). The schedule was established in May 1995 and is administered by the U.S. Army Corps of Engineers.

Approach

The emerging field of data mining addresses the issue of extracting information from large databases. Data mining is composed of several technologies that include signal processing, advanced statistics, multidimensional visualization, chaos theory, and machine learning. Machine learning is a field of artificial intelligence in which computer programs are developed that automatically learn cause-and-effect relations from example cases and data. For numerical data, commonly used learning methods include ANNs, genetic algorithms, multivariate adaptive regression splines, and partial and ordinary least squares.

A number of previous studies by the authors and others have used data mining to predict hydrodynamic and water-quality behaviors in the Beaufort, Cooper, Savannah, and Waccamaw River estuaries of South Carolina and Georgia (Roehl and others, 2000; Conrads and others, 2003; Conrads and others, 2006; and Conrads and Roehl, 2007) and stream temperatures in western Oregon (Risley and others, 2003). Results from the previously developed ANN-based models demonstrate that ANN models, combined with data-mining techniques, are an effective approach for simulating complex hydrologic systems.

The ultimate goal of this investigation was to produce an effective model to simulate water level, specific conductance, and total phosphorous for a given set of hydrologic conditions. The variability of water levels and water quality in the Refuge is a result of many factors, including inflows and outflows to the canals, precipitation, evapotranspiration, and groundwater losses. The approach taken uses all available flow, water-level, specific conductance, and total phosphorous measurements from the individual gages and sampling sites since the water-quality sampling networks were begun in 1995. The modeling approach uses correlation functions that were synthesized directly from data to predict how water level, specific conductance, and total phosphorus at the measurement locations respond to changing precipitation, evapotranspiration, inflow, and outflow conditions. In order to simulate the dynamic response of water levels and water quality, empirical models were developed to predict water level, specific conductance, and phosphorus for selected gages throughout the Refuge. Extensive continuous hydrologic datasets as well as data from extensive periodic sampling networks were available for the Refuge. Empirical water-level, specific conductance, and total phosphorus models were developed directly from these data by using data-mining techniques and ANN models.

The application of data-mining techniques to build empirical models to simulate the water levels, specific conductance, and total phosphorus was undertaken in three phases: (1) obtaining and evaluating the suitability of the hydrologic and water-quality data for developing empirical models; (2) developing models to simulate the water level at six streamgaging stations, specific conductance at 25 sampling locations, and total phosphorus at 14 sampling locations; and (3) developing a DSS that integrates historical databases, model controls, and model output into a spreadsheet application with a graphical user interface that allows the user to simulate scenarios of interest.

Data-Collection Networks

Many resource entities have collected data in the Refuge, including the USFWS, USGS, SFWMD, and local colleges and universities. Continuous hydrologic and meteorological data of water level, flow, precipitation, and evapotranspiration were collected in addition to water-quality sampling data of specific conductance and total phosphorus from various databases to build, train, and test the linear regression and ANN models for the LOXANN DSS. Descriptions and quality-assurance information of the available data-collection networks for the Refuge for the period 1995–2004 can be found in Meselhe and others (2005). Summaries and analyses of data collected by the Refuge can be found in the annual reports for its Enhanced Monitoring and Modeling Program (U.S. Fish and Wildlife Service 2007a, 2007b, and 2009).

The ideal dataset for developing empirical models for the Refuge would cover a large range of historical and contemporary climatic and operational conditions and have the temporal and spatial coverage to be able to characterize the hydrologic and water-quality dynamics throughout the Refuge. Typically, continuous data, such as water level or flow, are temporally dense (15-minute to 60-minute recording intervals) but can be spatially sparse. Conversely, water-quality sampling data (typically weekly or monthly sampling intervals) are usually more temporally sparse but often have a denser spatial coverage than continuous data. Extensive water-quality sampling began in 1995, and the period of record from 1995 to 2006 provides the most concurrent continuous hydrologic data, including data from the water-quality sampling networks. A description of the datasets used in the development of LOXANN DSS follows.

Continuous daily hydrologic data included inflows, outflows, water levels, precipitation, and evapotranspiration (fig. 6; table 1). The flow data represent the 19 hydrologic control structures around the perimeter canal and were characterized by their direction of flow—into or out of the Refuge or bidirectionally. Water-level data were collected from six USGS streamgaging stations; one of the gaging stations was proximal to the canal (site 1-8C) and the other five stations were located in the interior marsh. Streamgaging stations north and south were installed in 2001 and did not cover the period of record. Precipitation and weather data were recorded at 16 stations: 1 was in the marsh, 6 were along the canal, and 9 were outside of the Refuge. Evapotranspiration data were available at three of the weather stations. Pan evaporation data were available at station S5A, located on the canal at the northern tip of the Refuge. Evapotranspiration data were available at station STA1W to the northwest, and potential evapotranspiration data were available at station LOXWS located midway along the L-40 canal on the eastern side of the Refuge.

Table 1. Flow, water level, precipitation, and evapo-transpiration stations used in the model development.

[UTM, Universal Transverse Mercator; x, easting; y, northing; NAD83, North American Datum 1983; STA, stormwater treatment area]

Structure	Location	UTM x (NAD83)	UTM y (NAD83)
Flow data			
S-5A	L-7 Canal	562923.80	2951648.41
S-5AS	L-40 Canal	562923.80	2951648.41
G-300	L-40 Canal	563360.30	2950824.02
G-301	L-7 Canal	561649.23	2950621.87
G-310	L-7 Canal	555156.76	2942060.02
G-251	L-7 Canal	555557.05	2942007.13
S-6	L-7 Canal	555237.83	2928059.96
S-10E	L-39 Canal	555664.38	2927348.19
G-338	L-39 Canal	555293.06	2927854.37
S-10D	L-39 Canal	561683.30	2918858.31
S-10C	L-39 Canal	564597.91	2917008.87
S-10A	L-39 Canal	568592.55	2915744.44
S-39	L-39 Canal	570050.07	2915284.57
S-362	L-40 Canal	568081.26	2944903.95
ACME #1	L-40 Canal	570829.38	2943161.99
ACME #2	L-40 Canal	572508.66	2941521.83
G-94C	L-40 Canal	576431.10	2935866.25
G-94B	L-40 Canal	577582.06	2929275.93
G-94A	L-40 Canal	576780.29	2924092.71
Water level			
Site 1-7	Central marsh	565061.88	2933415.39
Site 1-8T	Central marsh	577474.80	2931309.20
Site 1-8C	Marsh site near canal	575029.51	2932854.66
Site 1-9	Central marsh	570077.53	2927288.80
North	Northern marsh	564356.19	2941626.14
South	Southern marsh	565752.41	2922897.27
Precipitation			
S-5A	L-7 Canal	562923.80	2951648.41
S-6	L-7 Canal	555237.83	2928059.96
S-39	L-39 Canal	570050.07	2915284.57
LOXWS	L-40 Canal	577503.46	2931177.16
Gage 6	Near L-40 Canal	57365.10	2908757.60
Gage 8	Near L-40 Canal	570877.40	2943262.60
WCA1ME	Central marsh	568748.3	2932450.2
Evapotranspiration data			
STA1W	STA-1W	556983.50	2946136.81

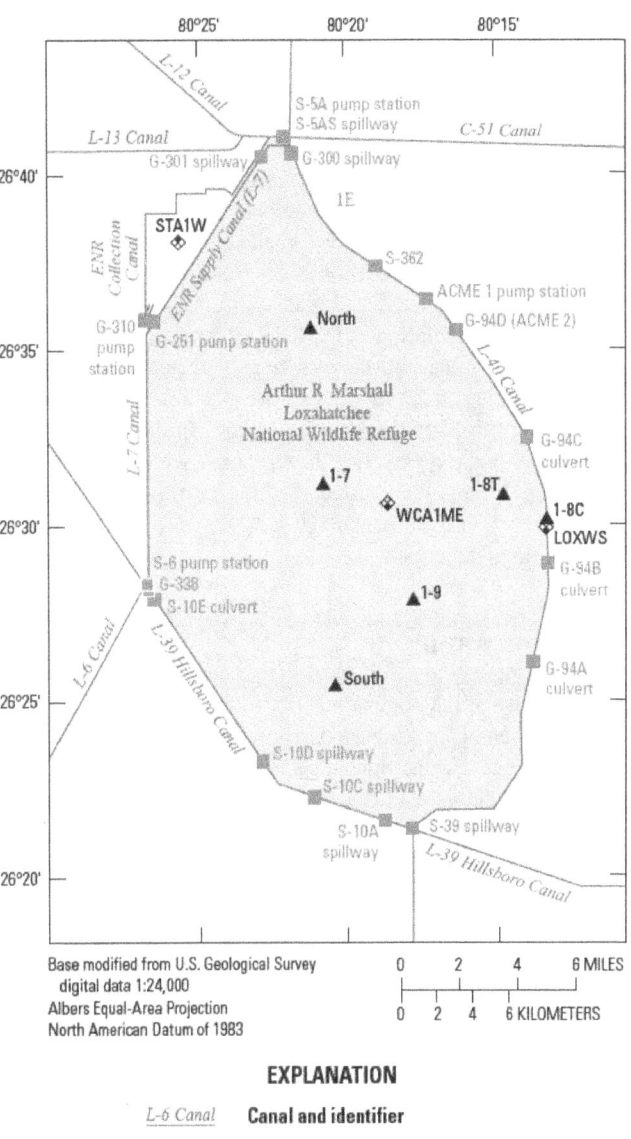

EXPLANATION

L-6 Canal	**Canal and identifier**
G-301 spillway ■	**Control structure and identifier**
	Continuous monitor site and identifier
◈ STA1W	Evapotranspiration
◈ LOXWS	Precipitation
▲ 1-9	Continuous streamgaging station

Figure 6. Location of weather and continuous water-level stations and flow-control structures, Arthur R. Marshall Loxahatchee National Wildlife Refuge, Florida.

Specific conductance and total phosphorus data were obtained from three sampling networks maintained by SFWMD—the Everglades Protection Area (EVPA) water-quality monitoring sites, the District Transects monitoring network, or "XYZ" data network (fig. 7; table 2), and from the hydraulic structures. Fourteen sampling sites in the EVPA network (also referred to as the "LOX" sites) were used to monitor the physical, chemical, and biological properties. The sampling interval generally was monthly but was variable depending on hydrologic conditions and site classification. From 1995 to 2008, at least 65 samples were collected from each site. The XYZ network was made up of 11 sampling sites along the southwestern portion of the Refuge and was established to measure the nutrient gradient from the L-39 canal into the marsh. Sampling of the XYZ sites was irregular. From 1995 to 2006, at least 68 samples were collected from each site. Water-quality sampling data were available for 15 of the hydraulic control structures in the Refuge. Similar to the other water-quality networks, the structures were sampled irregularly. From 1995 to 2006, the number of samples varied from 3 to 597, and more than 100 samples were collected at many of the structures.

Data Preparation

Because of the large number of hydrologic inputs to the Refuge, much of the flow and precipitation time-series data were aggregated to facilitate the analysis and modeling of the data. The flow data from the 19 control structures were aggregated into six flow groups (fig. 8). Aggregating data has the advantages of reducing the number of variables and diminishing spurious correlations between large and small flows from nearby hydraulic structures. Rainfall data were highly temporally and spatially variable and none of the precipitation time-series records were complete. A composite daily rainfall time-series record was computed by averaging the data from the six rain gages closest to the Refuge. If data from one or more of the gages were missing, the average was computed for the remaining gages. In addition, the rainfall values were converted to flow units for the Refuge. Assuming a Refuge area of 221 square miles, daily rainfall in inches was converted to cubic feet per second.

Limitations of the Historical Datasets

As with any modeling effort, empirical or deterministic, the accuracy of the model is dependent on the quality and quantity of the data and range of measured conditions used for training or calibrating the model. The available period of record for the hydrologic and water-quality data-collection networks can limit the range of water-level and water-quality conditions that the model can accurately simulate. Although data were available from the networks in the Refuge from the mid-1990s, the data were not always of a sufficient quality to use for developing empirical models. Environmental monitoring technology has changed substantially over the last 15 years. Periods of missing continuous data, especially flow and water-level data, limit the periods when the net flow into and out of the Refuge is known and when accurate models can be developed. Water-quality monitoring networks typically are established to meet regulatory compliance requirements and often provide sufficient long-term data to evaluate the status and trends of water-quality constituents of concern. Unfortunately, irregularly sampled water-quality data usually do not adequately capture the dynamic variability of complex systems, which is needed to develop accurate dynamic models. Specific limitations with the data collected for the Refuge to develop the LOXANN DSS are as follows.

- The flow data for control structures G-94A, G-94B, and G-94C (aggregated into Q5) were missing from January 1, 1996, until April 15, 2000. The data that were available indicate that at times these flow-control structures substantially affect the net flow; therefore, the data used to develop models were limited to the period after April 15, 2000.

- The south and north water-level stations were established in 2001. The shorter period of record, as compared to the other water-level sites, limited the data available for developing water-level models for all the sites.

- The temporal record for the flows, gage height, specific conductance, and total phosphorus was incomplete, and the specific conductance and total phosphorus measurements were particularly sparse. The water-quality sampling occurred on a small percentage of the days for which there were corresponding hydrologic data from 1995 to 2006. Of the 39 water-quality sampling sites, 32 sites had water-quality samples for 5 percent or less of the days. The site with the greatest number of water-quality samples, control structure S6, only had concurrent samples with hydrologic data for 21 percent of the days. In addition, many of the samples were not measured on the same day. This type of low frequency, nonconcurrent sampling generally is insufficient to represent the dynamics of a complex system. Data from the control structures typically would be used to provide boundary conditions for the water-quality variability at interior sampling sites.

Table 2. Water-quality sampling sites used in the model development.

[UTM, Universal Transverse Mercator; x, easting; y, northing; NAD83, North American Datum 1983]

Site	UTM x (NAD83)	UTM y (NAD83)
Everglades Protection Area		
LOX10	557696.533	2934097.335
LOX11	570618.481	2927057.254
LOX12	561819.067	2923516.529
LOX13	569763.753	2922876.125
LOX14	575259.851	2920565.147
LOX15	564635.159	2918366.964
LOX16	569209.115	2917240.300
LOX3	564139.639	2941524.321
LOX4	570207.126	2942378.775
LOX5	563950.427	2937560.441
LOX6	576727.276	2931944.920
LOX7	572077.711	2933267.939
LOX8	565964.015	2933883.533
LOX9	561072.830	2934147.524
South Florida Water Management District transect (XYZ)		
X0	555310.239	2929595.537
X1	555598.128	2929630.011
X2	556387.674	2930041.048
X3	557377.266	2929612.387
X4	559509.952	2930085.087
Y4	559573.425	2927366.295
Z1	555808.002	2927668.322
Z2	557023.968	2927256.124
Z3	558953.035	2926574.838
Z4	560964.178	2925240.763
Control structures		
S-5A	562923.797	2951648.413
G-300	563360.301	2950824.018
G-301	561649.234	2950621.874
G-310	555156.761	2942060.022
S-6	555237.829	2928059.963
S-10E	555664.380	2927348.193
S-10D	561683.299	2918858.313
S-10C	564597.907	2917008.867
S-10A	568592.553	2915744.442
S-39	570050.073	2915284.569
ACME #1	570829.375	2943161.990
ACME #2	572508.664	2941521.829
G-94C	576431.096	2935866.250
G-94B	577582.057	2929275.929

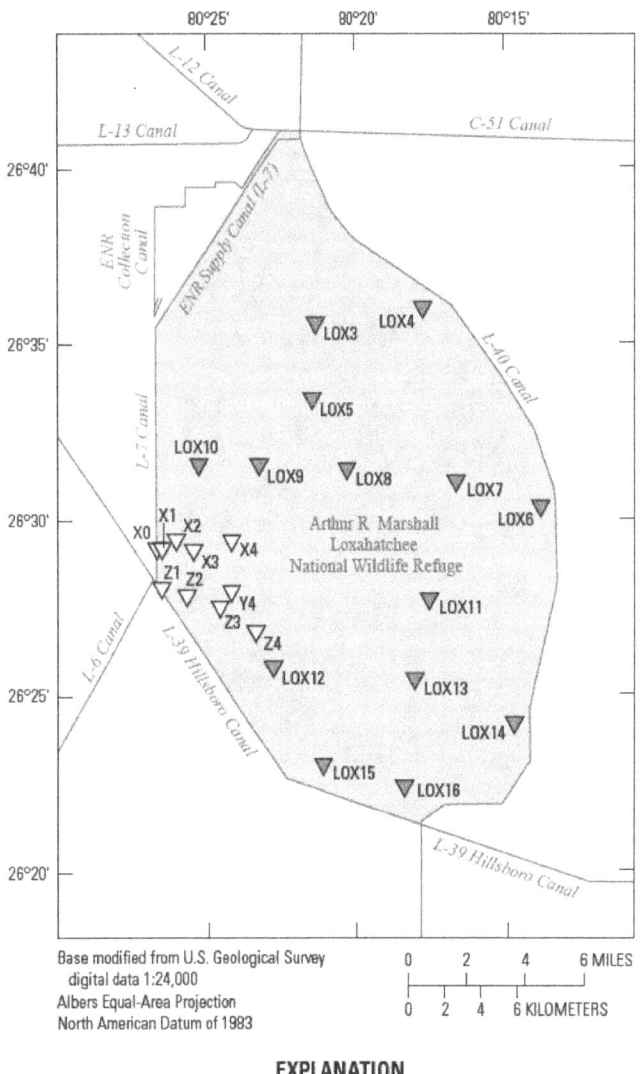

EXPLANATION

L-6 Canal Canal and identifier

Water-quality sampling site and identifier

▽LOX12   EVPA

▽Z4   XYZ

Figure 7. Location of District transect water-quality monitoring network (XYZ) and the Everglades Protection Area (EVPA) network, Arthur R. Marshall Loxahatchee National Wildlife Refuge, Florida.

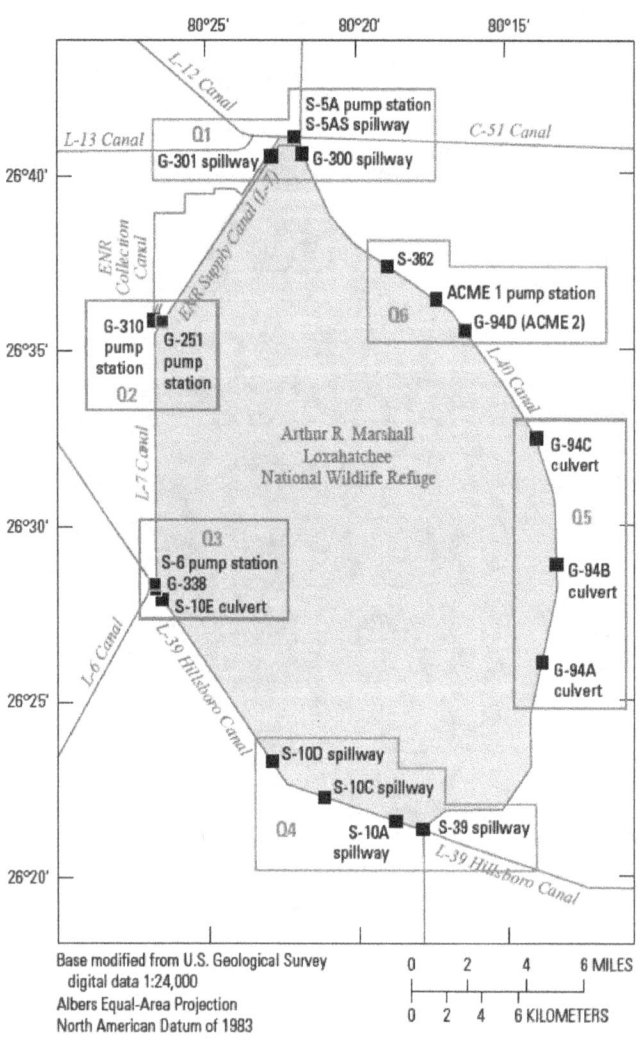

Figure 8. Flow-control structures and aggregation of structures (magenta) used in the analysis and model development, Arthur R. Marshall Loxahatchee National Wildlife Refuge, Florida.

Characterization of Marsh and Canal Water Levels

The primary sources for water levels in the Refuge marsh are precipitation and inflow and outflows from the control structures (U.S. Fish and Wildlife Service, 2000). The water levels at the six marsh sites are highly correlated and show similar dynamic responses to each other (fig. 9; table 3). Note that the length of record for stations north and south was much shorter than for the other four stations. Site 1-8C, the gage closest to a canal, shows the greatest dynamic variability. Three marsh gages, site 1-8T, site 1-9, and south, were highly correlated with coefficients of determinations, R^2s, from 0.94 to 0.97 (table 3). The high correlation is due to their proximity to canals. The relatively lower correlated stations, sites 1-8C and 1-7 (R^2 of 0.77), reflect the dampening effect of the water-level variability from the canal to the interior marsh. The lowest correlated stations, north and south (R^2 of 0.73), reflect the gradient of the drier northern section and wetter southern section of the Refuge.

Correlation analyses between the inputs (rainfall and control-structure flows) and response variable (water level) was performed to understand how the sources of water dynamically affect water levels. The timing effects that rainfall and flow inputs have on the water levels was analyzed by computing time delays, moving window averages, and time derivatives of rainfall, control-structure flows, and water levels. Although rainfall is a major source of water for the Refuge, the correlation, measured by R^2, between daily rainfall and daily water level is very low—less than 0.01 at the six water-level stations (table 4). The water level in the Refuge is a result of inputs from many sources over many temporal scales. To compare rainfall and water levels on a similar temporal scale, *the change* in daily water level and the daily rainfall, the correlations increased the R^2 for the five interior water-level stations to more than 0.20 and the canal station to 0.14 (table 4; fig. 10). Using a 2-day average rainfall instead of a daily rainfall further increased the correlation with the 1-day change in water level to between 0.34 and 0.59.

Rainfall not only has a short-term effect on water level as seen in the correlation with 1-day and 2-day changes in water levels, but also has an effect on long-term water levels. The cycles of the dry and wet seasons in South Florida are characterized by reduced rainfall between March and July and increased rainfall between August and February. This cycle also is seen in the seasonal water-level hydrograph with minimum water levels occurring in the late spring/summer (May or June) and maximum water levels occurring in the fall (October or November). The long-term dynamic between rainfall and water level can be seen by correlating moving window averages of rainfall with daily water levels. As the averaging window increases for rainfall, the correlation to water level increases until a maximum is reached. The

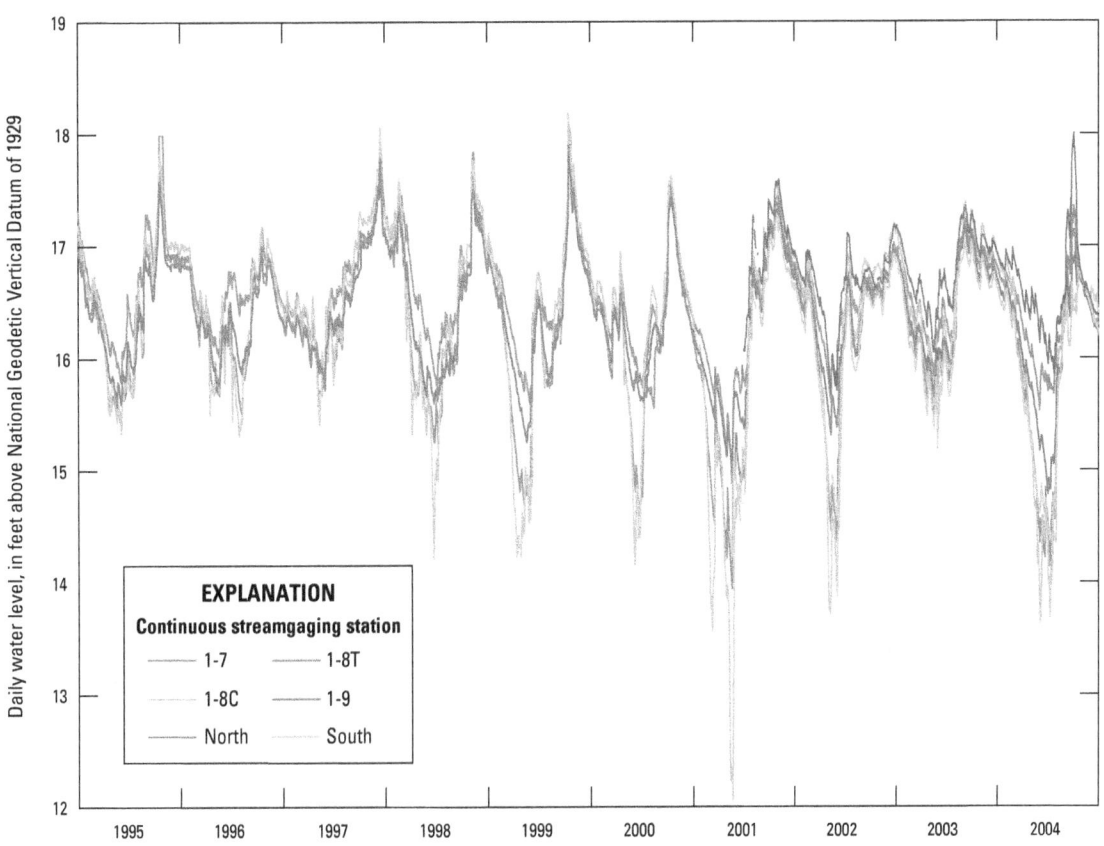

Figure 9.   Daily water levels for six continuous streamgaging stations, Arthur R. Marshall Loxahatchee National Wildlife Refuge, Florida, January 1995 to December 2004. See figure 6 for site locations.

Table 3.   Count, minimum, maximum, mean, standard deviations, and coefficient of determination of six water-level gages in the Refuge between 1995 and 2008.

Stream-gaging station	Count	Minimum	Maximum	Mean	Standard deviation	Coefficient of determination					
		Feet				Site 1-7	Site 1-8T	Site 1-8C	Site 1-9	North	South
Site 1-7	3,653	14.88	18.12	16.55	0.47	1.00	0.85	0.77	0.91	0.91	0.87
Site 1-8T	3,646	13.94	18.03	16.26	0.70	0.85	1.00	0.95	0.94	0.78	0.97
Site 1-8C	3,565	12.06	18.19	16.31	0.87	0.77	0.95	1.00	0.85	0.79	0.92
Site 1-9	3,653	14.78	17.90	16.35	0.51	0.91	0.94	0.85	1.00	0.81	0.95
North	1,261	15.67	18.00	16.73	0.38	0.91	0.78	0.79	0.81	1.00	0.73
South	1,304	14.23	17.27	16.10	0.72	0.87	0.97	0.92	0.95	0.73	1.00

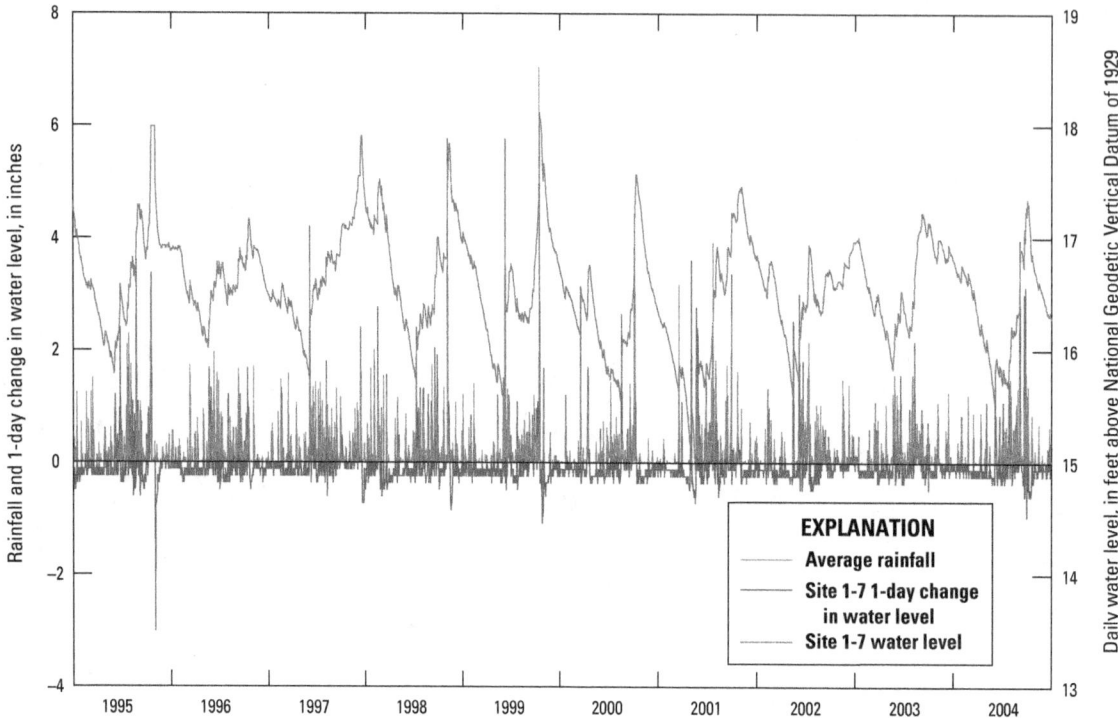

Figure 10. Average daily rainfall and the 1-day change in water level at site 1-7, and daily water level at site 1-7, Arthur R. Marshall Loxahatchee National Wildlife Refuge, Florida, January 1995 to December 2004. See figure 6 for site location.

Table 4. Coefficient of determination of daily water level and average rainfall, 1-day change in water level, and 2-day change in water level.

[R^2, coefficient of determination]

Stream-gaging station	R^2 of daily water level and daily rainfall	R^2 of 1-day change in water level and daily rainfall	R^2 of 1-day change in water level and 2-day average rainfall
Site 1-7	0.00	0.27	0.59
Site 1-8T	0.00	0.21	0.46
Site 1-8C	0.00	0.14	0.34
Site 1-9	0.00	0.25	0.54
North	0.00	0.26	0.46
South	0.00	0.22	0.49

220-day moving window average rainfall is plotted with the daily water level for the period 1995–2004 in figure 11. The R^2 between the two time series is 0.66. The transformation of the rainfall time series captures the majority of the interannual water-level variability between the dry and wet seasons.

A similar analysis can be performed for the control structures to evaluate correlation between flow releases (both inflows and outflows) and rainfall and the correlation of flow releases and water levels. The correlation between the optimal moving window average (highest R^2) of flow at control structures and rainfall is presented in table 5. Only control structures with R^2 greater than 0.10 are listed. The R^2s and moving window sizes in table 5 provide some insight to the operations of the control structures. The control structures with the higher R^2s have a higher response to recent rainfall inputs, and their operations are more connected with rainfall than the structures with lower R^2s that are operated with less regard for recent rainfall conditions. The structures with moving window average sizes less than 8 days are inflow control structures. The structures with higher moving window average sizes greater than 15 days are outflow structures. The difference in these moving window sizes indicates that water from rainfall events moves into the Refuge faster than water that is released from control structures in the Refuge.

The correlation among the control-structure flows, rainfall, and water levels can be analyzed to show a relative proportioning of the influence of flows and rainfall on water levels. The aggregated flows (fig. 8) and rainfall R^2s, time delays, and moving window sizes are presented in table 6. The use of time derivatives is a common analytical method for analyzing the dynamics of a system. Often time delays exist between when an event is measured and the time that the response is observed in a system. Modeling a system is more complicated when two events of interest, a cause and an effect, do not occur simultaneously. The time between cause and effect is called the "time delay" or "delay." Each input variable of a model has its own delay. Determining the correct

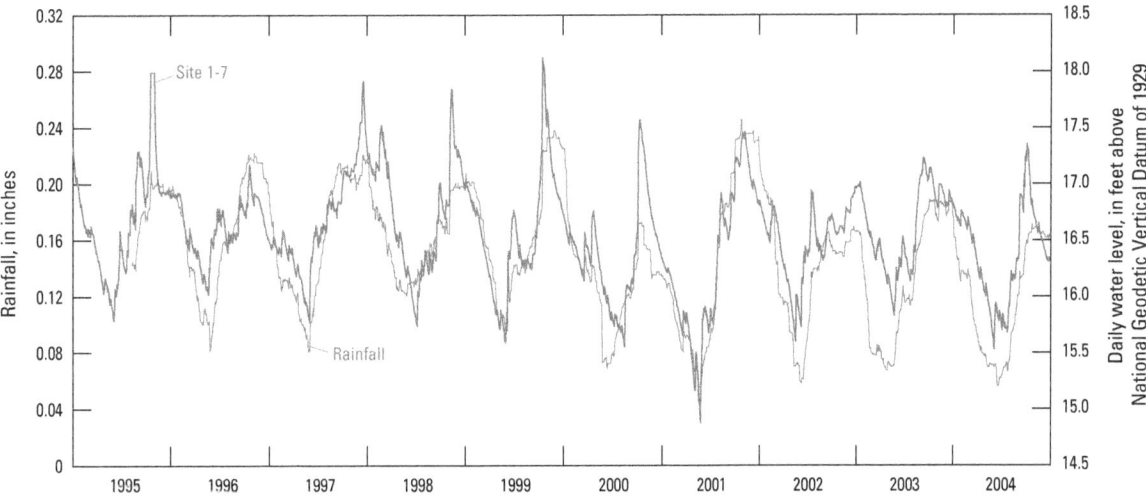

Figure 11. Two-hundred-twenty-day moving window average of rainfall and daily water level at site 1-7, Arthur R. Marshall Loxahatchee National Wildlife Refuge, Florida, January 1995 to December 2004. See figure 6 for site location.

Table 5. Flow structure, aggregated flow group assignment, moving window average, and coefficient of determination between daily rainfall and flow.

[MWA, moving window average; R^2, coefficient of determination]

Structure	Aggregated flow group	MWA	R^2
G-300	Q1	4	0.15
G-301	Q1	5	0.12
S-6	Q3	6	0.43
S-5A	Q1	6	0.36
ACME #2	Q6	8	0.37
ACME #1	Q6	8	0.35
G-310	Q2	8	0.28
S-362	Q6	11	0.48
S-10A	Q4	15	0.30
S-10D	Q4	23	0.42
S-10C	Q4	23	0.39

time delays for pulses and the system response is critical to accurately simulate a dynamic system. For example, a control structure may release a pulse of water and the water levels at a station in a canal may respond immediately (a time delay of zero) or there may be a 1- or 2-day delay in the response to water levels at an interior marsh station (time delays of one and two, respectively). The time delays are computed by incrementally lagging the input time series and determining the peak correlation with the response variable. Because of the shorter period of record for stations north and south, they are not included in this correlation analysis.

The 1-day change in water level at the two interior marsh sites, sites 1-7 and 1-9, are more correlated with rainfall than the site 1-8T and site 1-8C stations (fig. 6). The four water-level stations are most responsive to the aggregated Q1 and Q3 flows with a 1-day time delay (fig. 8). The stations have a 2-day time delay for the Q2 flows. All of the stations have negative time delays for the Q4 flows, which are flows out of the system. Site 1-8C is fastest to respond to releases with a time delay of 1 day. Site 1-7 is the slowest station to respond to releases from the canal with a 7-day delay.

Table 6. Coefficient of determination, time delay, and moving window average between the 1-day change in water level and rainfall and aggregated flows.

[R^2, coefficient of determination; τ, time delay; MWA, moving window average; Q#, aggregated flow assignment]

Stream-gaging station	Rainfall			Q1			Q2			Q3			Q4			Q5			Q6		
	R^2	τ	MWA	R^2	τ	MWA	R^2	τ	MWA	R^2	τ	MWA	R^2	τ	MWA	R^2	τ	MWA	R^2	τ	MWA
Site 1-7	0.59	0	2	0.23	1	1	0.05	2	1	0.24	1	1	0.02	−7	8	0.03	1	1	0.12	1	1
Site 1-8C	0.34	0	2	0.14	1	2	0.04	2	2	0.17	1	2	0.03	−1	2	0.05	0	1	0.10	0	1
Site 1-8T	0.46	0	2	0.16	1	1	0.04	2	1	0.19	1	1	0.03	−3	1	0.04	1	1	0.09	1	1
Site 1-9	0.55	0	2	0.19	1	1	0.05	2	1	0.22	1	2	0.02	−3	2	0.04	1	1	0.12	1	2

Simulating Water Levels, Specific Conductance, and Total Phosphorus

Simulating water level, specific conductance, and total phosphorus typically is done using dynamic deterministic models that incorporate the mathematical descriptions of the physics of the hydrodynamics and water chemistry of surface-water systems. These one-, two-, or three-dimensional models often require extensive data collection and are time consuming to apply to hydrologic systems. Although mechanistic models have been the state of the practice for regulatory evaluations of anthropogenic effects on hydrologic systems, developments in the field of advanced statistics, machine learning, and data mining offer opportunities to develop empirical ANN models that are often more accurate. Conrads and Roehl (1999) compared the application of a deterministic model and an ANN model to simulate dissolved-oxygen concentrations for the tidally affected Cooper River in South Carolina. They found that the ANN models offer some important advantages, including faster development time, utilization of larger amounts of data, the incorporation of optimization routines, and model dissemination in spreadsheet applications. With the real-time streamgaging network and water-quality sampling network for the Refuge and the availability of large databases of hydrologic and water-quality data, the USGS and the USFWS realized an opportunity existed to develop an empirical model using data-mining techniques, including ANNs, to simulate water level, specific conductance, and total phosphorus in the Refuge.

Artificial Neural Networks

Models generally fall into one of two categories: deterministic (or mechanistic) or empirical. Deterministic models are created from first-principles equations, whereas empirical modeling adapts generalized mathematical functions to fit a line or surface through data from one or more variables. The most common empirical approach is ordinary least squares (OLS), which relates variables using straight lines, planes, or hyper-planes, whether the actual relations are linear or not. Calibrating either type of model attempts to optimally synthesize a line or surface through the observed data. Calibrating models is difficult when data have substantial measurement error or are incomplete, or when the variables for which data are available provide only a partial explanation of the causes of variability. The principal advantages that empirical models, such as ANN models, have over deterministic models are that they can be developed much faster and are more accurate when the modeled systems are well characterized by data. Empirical models, however, are prone to problems when poorly applied. Overfitting and multicollinearity caused by correlated input variables can lead to invalid mappings between input and output variables (Roehl and others, 2003).

An ANN model is a flexible mathematical structure capable of describing complex nonlinear relations between input and output datasets. The structure of ANN models is loosely based on the biological nervous system with interconnections of neurons and synapses (Hinton, 1992). Although numerous types of ANN models exist, the most commonly used type of ANN is the multilayer perceptron (Rosenblatt, 1958). As shown in figure 12, multilayer perceptron ANNs are constructed from layers of interconnected processing elements called neurons, each executing a simple "transfer function." All input layer neurons are connected to every hidden layer neuron, and every hidden layer neuron is connected to every output neuron. Multiple hidden layers are possible, but a single layer is sufficient for most problems.

Typically, linear transfer functions are used to scale input values from the input layer to the hidden layer and generally fall within the range that corresponds to the most linear part of the s-shaped sigmoid transfer functions used from the hidden layer to the output layer (fig. 12). Each connection has a "weight" w_i associated with it, which scales the output received by a neuron from a neuron in an antecedent layer. The output of a neuron is a simple combination of the values it receives through its input connections and their weights, and the neuron's transfer function.

An ANN is "trained" by iteratively adjusting its weights to minimize the error by which it maps inputs to outputs for a dataset composed of input/output vector pairs. Prediction accuracy during and after training can be measured by a number of metrics, including coefficient of determination (R^2) and root mean square error (RMSE). An algorithm that commonly is used to train multilayer perceptron ANNs is the back error propagation training algorithm (Rumelhart and others, 1986). Jensen (1994) describes the details of the multilayer perceptron ANN, the type of ANN used in this study. Multilayer perceptron ANNs can synthesize functions to fit high-dimension, nonlinear multivariate data. Devine and others (2003) and Conrads and Roehl (2005) describe their use of multilayer perceptron ANNs in multiple applications to model and control combined manmade and natural systems, including disinfection byproduct formation, industrial air emissions monitoring, and surface-water systems affected by point and nonpoint-source pollution.

Experimentation with a number of ANN model architectural and training parameters typically is part of the modeling process. For correlation analysis or predictive modeling applications, a number of candidate ANN models are trained and evaluated for their statistical accuracy and their representation of process physics. Interactions between combinations of variables also are considered along with the selection of the training dataset from the overall dataset. For models where there is a large dataset with good representation of the range of historical behaviors, a small percentage of the dataset (10–25 percent) may be selected for the training dataset. For problems with limited data, a larger percentage of the dataset (75–100 percent) may be used in the training

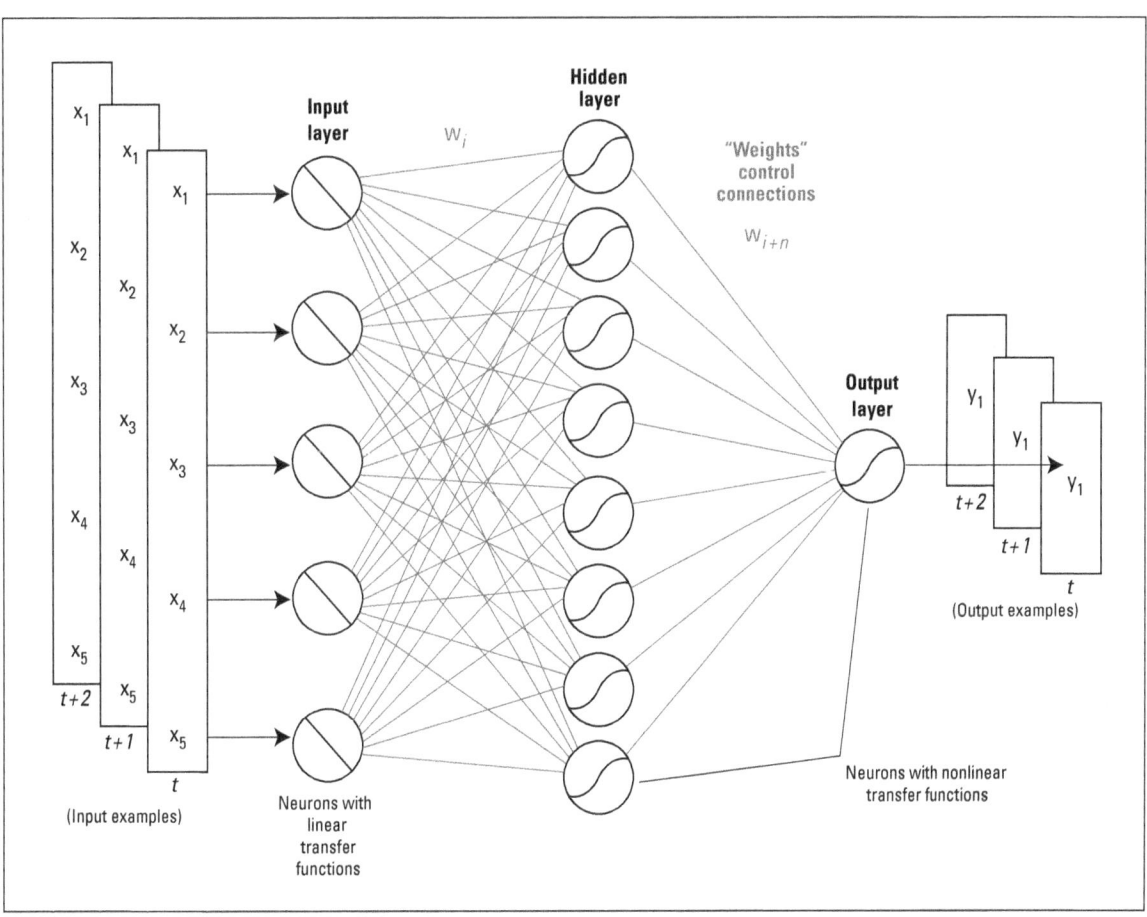

Figure 12. Multilayer perceptron artificial neural network architecture (from Conrads and Roehl, 2007).

dataset. Finally, a satisfactory model can be exported for end-user deployment. In general, a high-quality predictive model can be obtained when

- The data ranges are well distributed throughout the stated space of interest,

- The input variables selected by the modeler share "mutual information" about the output variables,

- The form "prescribed" or "synthesized" for the model used to "map" (correlate) input variables to output variables is a good one. Techniques such as OLS and physics-based finite-difference models prescribe the functional form of the model's fit of the calibration data. Machine-learning techniques like ANN models synthesize a best fit to the data.

Subdividing a complex modeling problem into sub-problems and then addressing each is an effective means of achieving the best possible results. A collection of submodels whose calculations are coordinated by a computer program constitutes a "super-model." For the Refuge investigation, daily linear regression and ANN models (submodels) were developed for water level, specific conductance, and total phosphorous at either continuous gages or at sampling sites. These submodels were then incorporated into a super-model application that integrates the model controls, model database, and model outputs. The super-model for the project is LOXANN DSS. The ANN models described in this report were developed using the iQuest™ data-mining software[3] (Version 2.03C DM Rev31). The ANN models were deployed in the DSS using the Visual Basic run-time library of the iQuest R/T™ software.

---

[3] The iQuest™ software is exclusively distributed by Advanced Data Mining, LLC, 3620 Pelham Road, PMB 351, Greenville, SC 29615-5044, Phone: (864) 201-8679, e-mail: info@advdatamining.com, *http //www.advdmi.com.*

Development of Water-Level, Specific Conductance, and Total Phosphorus Models

The data described above were used to develop empirical process models of the Refuge and are included in LOXANN DSS so that the user can run long-term simulations to evaluate permutations of the actual historical record. The LOXANN DSS models predict how rainfall, evapotranspiration, and flows into and out of the Refuge affect water levels at 6 sites, specific conductance at 25 sites, and total phosphorus at 14 sites. The water-level models are hybrid models that employ a linear least-squares regression and a nonlinear spatially interpolating ANN (SIANN) model. The specific conductance and total phosphorus models cascade from the predictions of the water-level model, but use only SIANN models. The overall architecture of the water-level, specific conductance, and total phosphorus models are shown in figure 13.

Statistical Measures of Prediction Accuracy

Statistical measures of prediction accuracy were computed for the water-level, specific conductance, and total phosphorus

values, and for the linear regression and SIANN models. The statistics for the water-level, specific conductance, and total phosphorus simulations capture the ability of the multistep modeling approaches to accurately estimate water levels at the streamgaging stations or specific conductance and total phosphorus at the XYZ and LOX sampling sites. The statistics for the linear regression and SIANN models (static, dynamic, and error correction models) document these intermediate models. Because several models are used, the statistics for the individual models may not be an indication of the quality of the final estimates. Ultimately, the water-level, specific conductance, and total phosphorus simulations should be evaluated by the statistics for the final simulation.

Model accuracy typically is reported in terms of R^2 and commonly is interpreted as the "goodness of the fit" of a model. An alternative interpretation is one of answering the question, "How much information does one variable or a group of variables provide about the behavior of another variable?" For example, in the first context, $R^2 = 0.6$ might be disappointing, whereas in the latter, it is merely an accounting of how much information is shared by the variables being used. The mean error and RMSE statistics provide a measure of the prediction accuracy of the ANN models. The mean error is a measure of the bias of model predictions—whether the

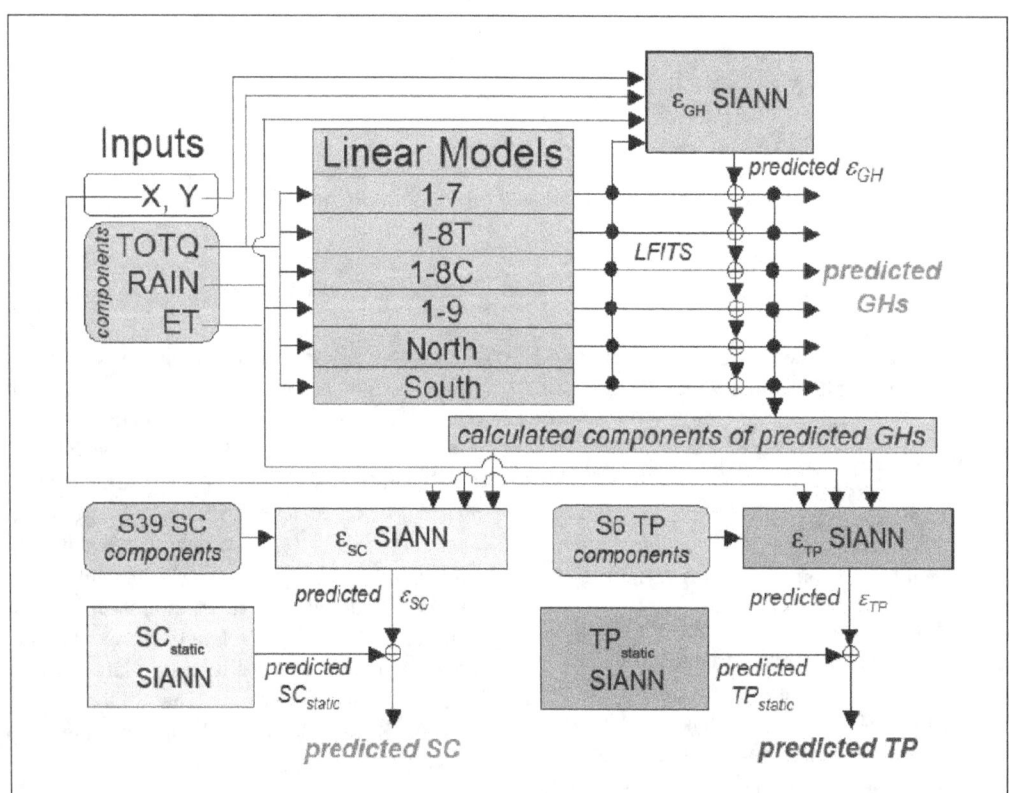

Figure 13.   Water-level, specific conductance (SC), and total phosphorus (TP) model architecture. Blue items denote input parameters that are calculated from measured data, user-inputs, and submodel output data. Green, yellow, and pink items are submodels used to predict water level, specific conductance, and total phosphorus, respectively.

model overpredicts or underpredicts the measured data. The mean error is presented as the adjustment to the simulated values to equal the measured values; therefore, a negative mean error indicates an oversimulation by the model, and a positive mean error indicates an underprediction by the ANN model. Mean errors near zero may be misleading because negative and positive discrepancies in the simulations can cancel each other. Root mean square error addresses the limitations of mean error by computing the magnitude, rather than the direction (sign) of the discrepancies. The units of the mean error and RMSE statistics are the same as the simulated variable of the model.

The accuracy of the models, as given by RMSE, should be evaluated with respect to the measured range of the output variable. The percent model error is the ratio of the RMSE to the range of the output measured data. A model may have a low RMSE, but if the range of the output variable is small, the model may only be accurate for a small range of conditions and the model error may be a relatively large percentage of the model response. For example, if the RMSE for a model is 0.5 foot (ft) and the measured range is 0–2 ft, the percent model error would be 25 percent. Likewise, a model may have a large RMSE, but if the range of the output variable is large, the model error may be a relatively small percentage of the total model response. For example, if the RMSE for a model is 2 ft and the measured range is 0–20 ft, the percent model error would be 10 percent.

Water-Level Models

The water-level model is composed of seven submodels. Six of the submodels use linear regression to predict water levels at sites 1-7, 1-8T, 1-8C, 1-9, north, and south. The seventh submodel is an ANN model that corrects a portion of the prediction error for each of the linear regression submodels. The notation for water level or gage height (used interchangeably) variables used in the models is "GH." The following steps describe the development and functions of the water-level submodels.

The first step is to convert model inputs into similar units. The daily averages of the aggregated flows Q1–Q6 in cubic feet per second are summed to a total flow (TOTQ, fig. 13). Total flow is converted into an estimated, spatially averaged daily change in water level in inches (TOTQ-inch) for all of the Refuge.

$$TOTQ\text{-}inch = TOTQ \text{ cubic feet per second}$$
$$\times\, 86{,}400 \text{ seconds per day} \times 1\,/\,(221 \text{ square miles})$$
$$\times (1/(5{,}280 \times 5{,}280 \text{ square feet per square mile}))$$
$$\times 12 \text{ inches per foot}$$

The second step is to create linear regression models for each water-level gage. A spreadsheet tool called the super tau tool was used to create linear statistical submodels ($y = mx + b$) that correlate rainfall (RAIN), evapotranspiration (ET), and total flow (TOTQ-inches) to each water-level time series (fig. 14). The user-controlled super tau tool computes

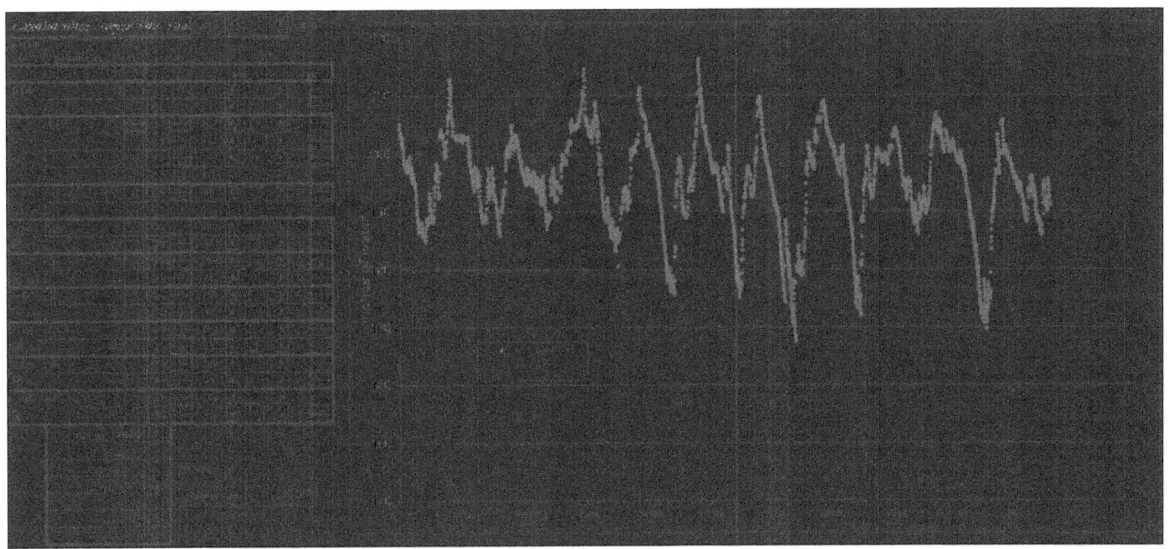

Figure 14. Screen capture of user interface of the super tau tool. The middle and upper left are user controls for selecting water-level site, input parameters, time delays, and moving window size. The lower left are summary statistics for the curve fit. Plot shows the measured data (blue) and the linear fit (yellow).

moving window averages for rainfall, evapotranspiration, and flows. The different moving window averages are used to represent different spectral components of the forces that modulate water-level behavioral dynamics. This process transforms the raw input signal into a waveform that is more correlated with a water-level signal and more representative of the input-output behavior of the physical process. An example of the linear fit for site 1-7 is shown in figure 15. Because all of the transformed parameters (rainfall and flow) are in units of inches, their sum (SUMQ) can be compared directly to a water-level signal. The super tau tool fits SUMQ linearly (water level = $m \times$ SUMQ + b) and nonlinearly (water level = $a \times \ln($SUMQ$)$).

Experimentation with different versions of the super tau tool indicated that it provides too many degrees of freedom, such that comparable curve-fit statistics can be obtained with significantly different input configurations, and that some water-level signals are better fit nonlinearly. Too many inputs to a model may overfit the data and result in poor predictive capabilities of the model. The number of inputs to the models was limited to decrease the degrees of freedoms and improve the predictive soundness of the final models. The three inputs to the model are evapotranspiration, rainfall, and inflows. The largely sinusoidal evapotranspiration time series characterizes seasonal and annual patterns and therefore was limited to one moving window average. Rainfall has a short- and long-range water-level response as seen in the correlations to daily changes in water level (fig. 10) and large moving window averages of rainfall and daily water levels (fig. 11). There, the

rainfall inputs were limited to two inputs. Similar to the rainfall inputs, it was decided to limit the Q1–Q6 inputs to two moving window averages to capture the shorter and longer range water-level responses to inflows. This effectively limited the number of inputs time series to five. The final water-level submodels were limited to only linear regressions derived from the mass balance of flow and rainfall (SUMQ). The residual error of these linear regression water-level models (ε_{GH}) was simulated with a nonlinear ANN. The residual error of the water-level models, ε_{GH}, is calculated by subtracting a predicted value from a measured value. Summing the outputs of the linear and ANN models yields statistically higher prediction accuracy.

The process by which moving window averages were set is described as follows. Evapotranspiration (ET) and flows (Q1–Q6) were set to zero and the two rainfall (RAIN) moving window averages were set to maximize the R^2 of the model. The two Q1–Q6 moving window averages were set to maximize R^2. Then, the one ET moving window average was set to further maximize R^2. After the initial setting of the moving window average sizes for the five input variables, some small adjustments to the moving window average sizes were made to arrive at a maximum R^2. Table 7 presents the window sizes and statistics of the linear water-level submodels for each site. It should be noted that rainfall gives the spikiest signal, followed by control-structure flows (TOTQ), with evapotranspiration (ET) being largely seasonally sinusoidal. Applying a moving window average changes a spiky signal more than it does a relatively smooth signal. Figure 16 shows the residual error, ε_{GH}, for linear regression water-level submodels.

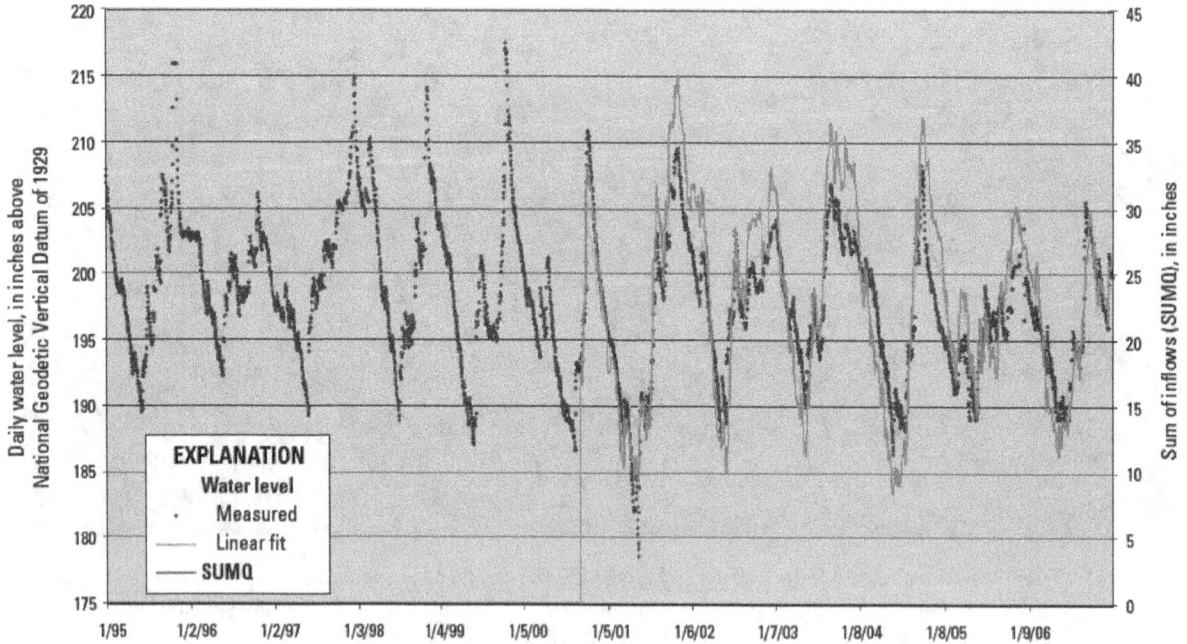

Figure 15.   Measured and linearly predicted daily water levels and SUMQ at site 1-7, Arthur R. Marshall Loxahatchee National Wildlife Refuge, Florida, January 1995 to January 2007. A 5-inch increment is used for both left and right axes. See figure 6 for location.

Table 7. Moving window averages for rainfall (RAIN1 and RAIN2), evapotranspiration (ET), and total flow (TOTQ-in 1 and TOTQ-in 2) inputs for six linear water-level models along with the slope, y-intercept, and coefficient of determination.

[MWA, moving window average; R^2, coefficient of determination]

Stream-gaging station	Count	RAIN1, MWA	RAIN2, MWA	ET, MWA	TOTQ-in 1, MWA	TOTQ-in 2, MWA	Slope	Y-intercept	R^2
Site 1-7	2,307	262	42	11	146	1	0.663	181.64	0.839
Site 1-8T	1,705	286	82	55	206	45	0.87	172.39	0.913
Site 1-8C	2,159	286	80	42	206	8	1.182	165.78	0.815
Site 1-9	2,312	265	45	39	141	1	0.731	181.15	0.867
North	1,985	289	51	5	140	1	0.619	182.88	0.753
South	1,436	264	58	14	233	19	0.993	165.23	0.933

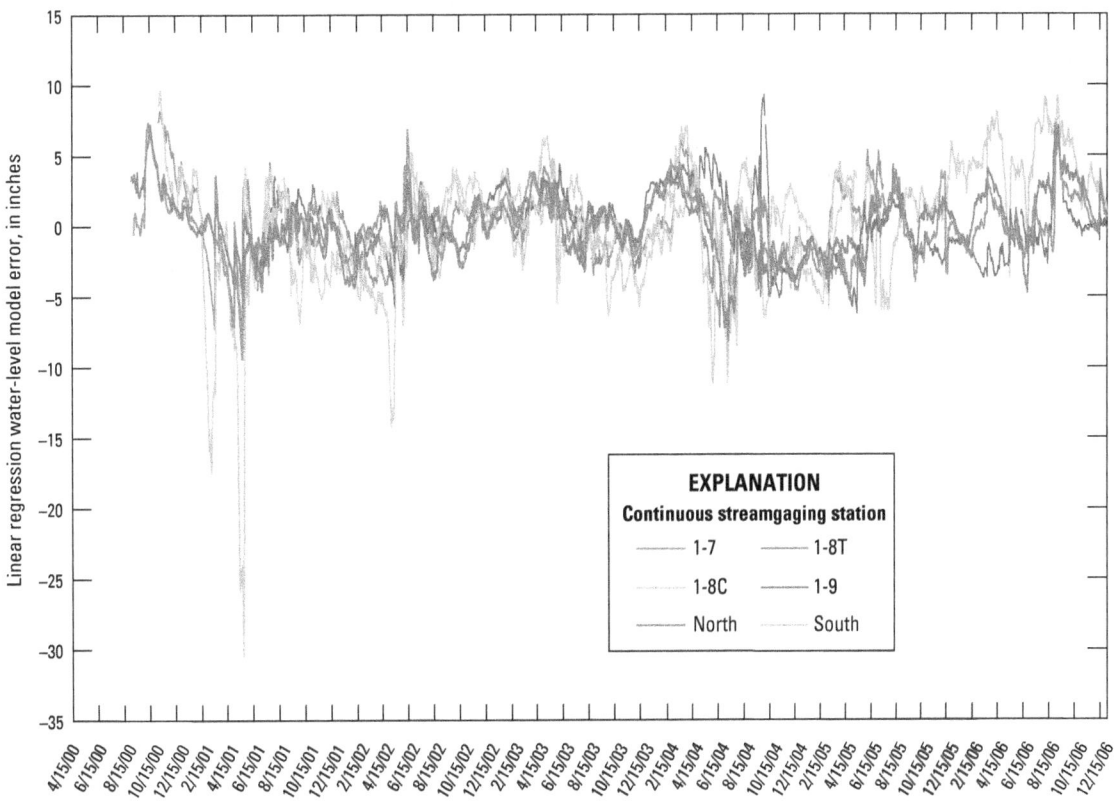

Figure 16. Linear regression water-level model errors for six continuous streamgaging stations, Arthur R. Marshall Loxahatchee National Wildlife Refuge, Florida, April 2000 to December 2006. See figure 6 for site locations.

The final step in simulating water levels is to create an error prediction model to increase the accuracy of the linear regression water-level models. A SIANN as described by Roehl and others (2006a) was developed to predict the residual errors (ε_{GH}) of the linear fit submodels (fig. 16). Here, a single SIANN is used to model the ε_{GH} signals for all the water-level sites. This approach uses a "stacked" dataset that includes time series and static variables (spatial coordinates) for the six water-level stations. The representation of the dynamic input signals is as follows. Moving window averages of 3, 10, 30, 90, 210, and 330 days were calculated for rainfall (RAIN), evapotranspiration (ET), and total inflow and outflow (TOTQ) and were named sequentially for the increasing moving window size. For example, RAIN_A0 represented the 3-day moving window average for rainfall, RAIN_A1 represented the 10-day average, RAIN_A2 represented the 30-day average, and so on. The moving window sizes were selected to capture daily, weekly, monthly, seasonal, intra-annual, and annual variability of the parameter. For each parameter, differences between each moving window average and the next larger window-sized moving window average were calculated, for example, RAIN_D0=RAIN_A0−RAIN_A1 and RAIN_D1=RAIN_A1−RAIN_A2 and so on. No differences were calculated for the 330-day moving window averages (fig. 17). This approach is analogous to band-pass spectral filtering in that it decomposes a raw signal into different spectral components. It is left to the SIANN to learn which

parameters and spectral ranges are the best predictors of behaviors that are manifest in ε_{GH} and which were not captured by the linear fit water-level models.

ANN models are developed iteratively by starting with a candidate pool of input parameters, training the ANN with them, and then using prediction accuracy statistics, such as R^2 and input-output sensitivities, to cull the least important inputs. Because of the spatial variability in water level among the sites, only ET_D3 was culled. The flow of data and linear model predictions into and out of the SIANN are shown in figure 13. The 20 inputs used in the final SIANN are listed below.

- GH-LFITS=the prediction made by the linear submodels at each site

- X, Y=coordinates of the water-level sites that have been normalized by subtracting the lowest UTM (Universal Transverse Mercator) coordinates of the Refuge's boundary

- RAIN_D0, RAIN_D1, RAIN_D2, RAIN_D3, RAIN_D4, RAIN_A5

- ET_D1, ET_D2, ET_D3, ET_D4, ET_A5

- TOTQ_D0, TOTQ_D1, TOTQ_D2, TOTQ_D3, TOTQ_D4, TOTQ_A5

Variable names and descriptions for all the input variables used in the LOXANN DSS are listed in appendix 1.

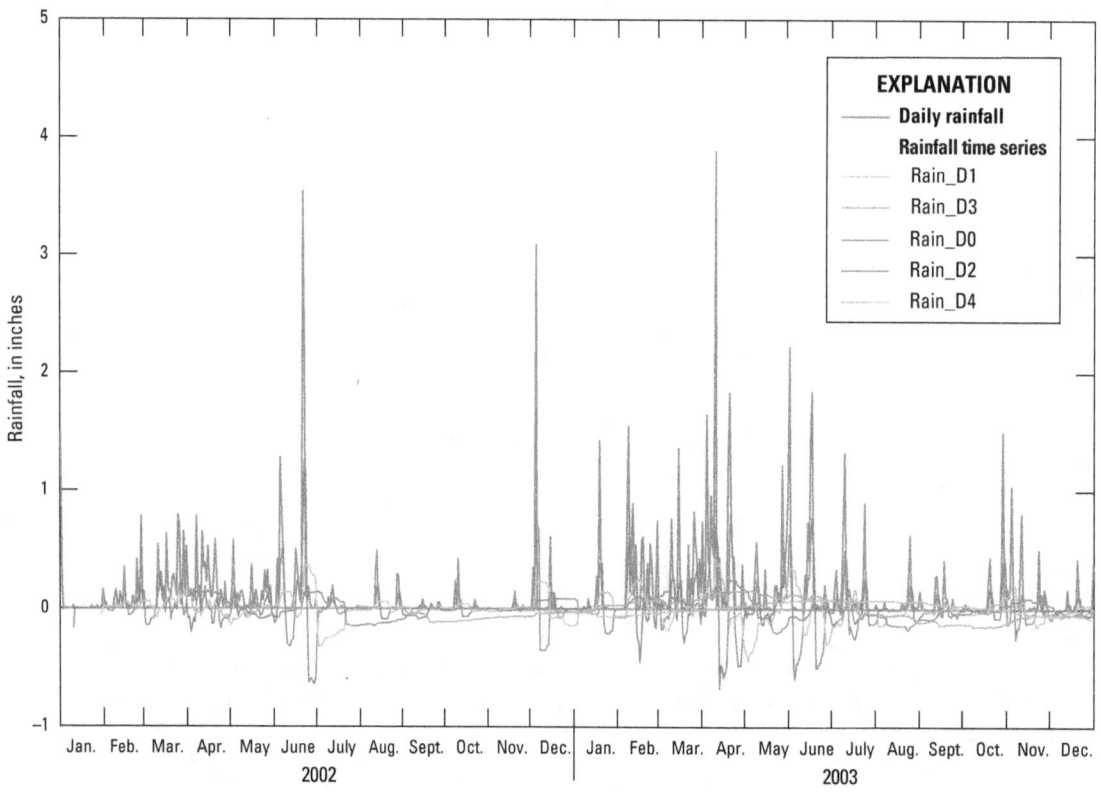

Figure 17.   Average daily rainfall and five frequency components for the rainfall time series, Arthur R. Marshall Loxahatchee National Wildlife Refuge, Florida, January 2002 to December 2003.

The SIANN was trained using approximately 50 percent of the available data, which were randomly selected, with the balance being set aside to test the submodel's prediction accuracy. Figure 18 shows the gage height error prediction (ε_{GH}) of the SIANN model. The stacked dataset used to train the SIANN model concatenates the data. The predictions for each gaging station are shown beside one another. Note in table 8 that the R^2 and RMSE of the training and test data are similar. The final water-level prediction is the combination of the linear water-level models prediction and the SIANN model error prediction for the site. The measured and simulated

water levels for the Refuge are shown in figure 19, and the water-level model performance statistics are listed in table 9.

After the development of the gage height models, it came to the authors' attention that there is an approximately 0.16 ft discrepancy between the water level at site 1-8C and the vertical datum (Michael Waldon, U.S. Fish and Wildlife Service, oral commun., January 7, 2010; fig. 20). This discrepancy does not affect the prediction of water level at site 1-8C but would affect analysis of water-level slopes between site 1-8C and the other five gaging stations. To account for this discrepancy, a –0.16 ft adjustment was made to the site 1-8C gage-height predictions.

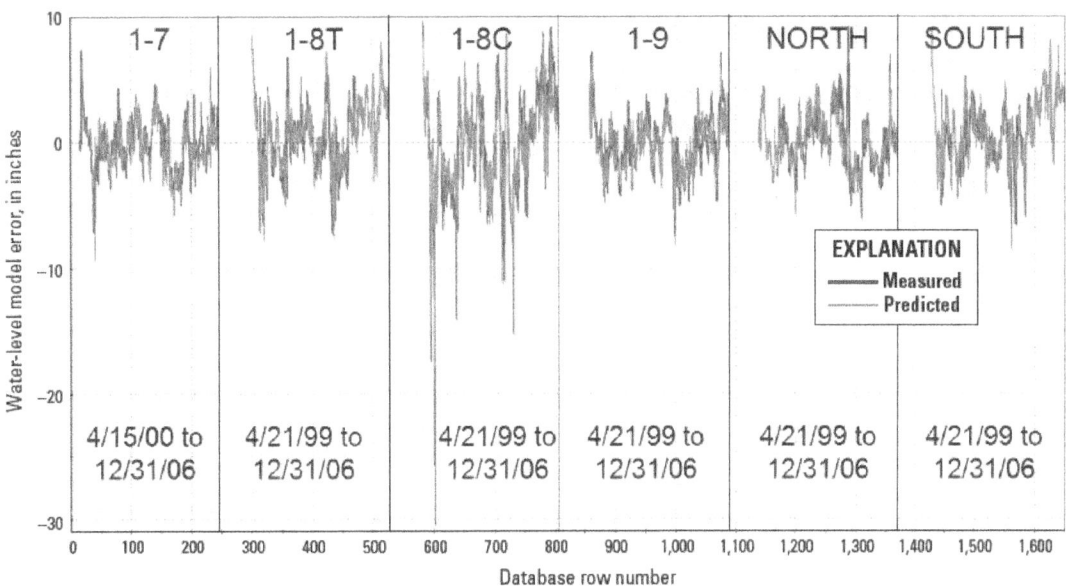

Figure 18. Measured and predicted water-level model error for six continuous streamgaging stations, Arthur R. Marshall Loxahatchee National Wildlife Refuge, Florida. See figure 6 for locations.

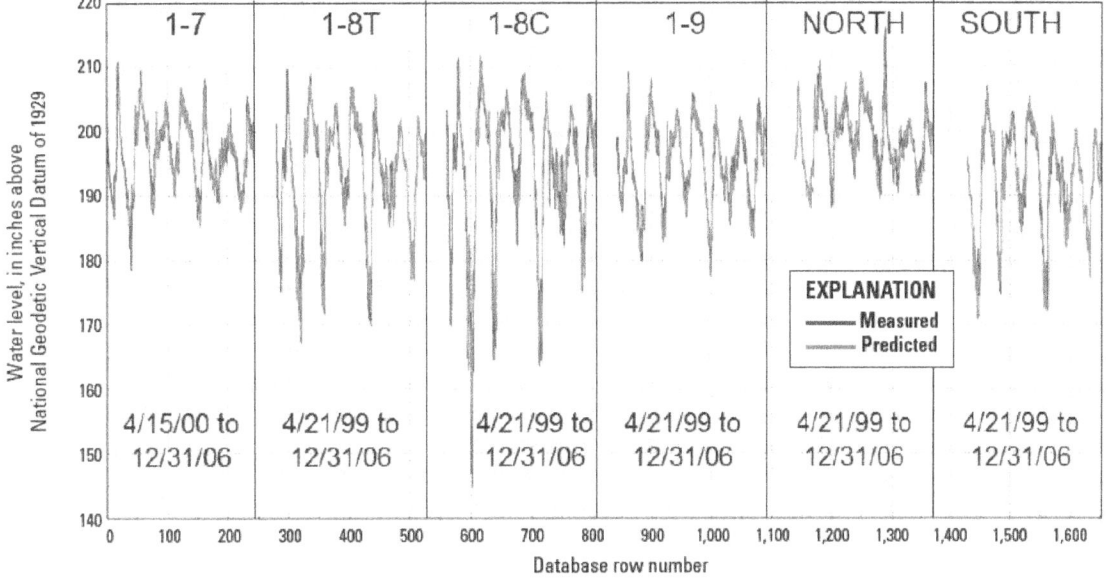

Figure 19. Measured and predicted water level for six continuous streamgaging stations, Arthur R. Marshall Loxahatchee National Wildlife Refuge, Florida. See figure 6 for locations.

Table 8. Water-level error correction model performance statistics.

[R², coefficient of determination; RMSE, root mean square error]

Dataset	Count	R²	RMSE inches
Training	5,847	0.72	1.46
Testing	5,873	0.73	1.52

Table 9. Statistics for final water-level simulations.

[R², coefficient of determination; RMSE, root mean square error]

Streamgaging station	Count	R²	RMSE	Minimum	Maximum	Range	Model error, percent
			Inches				
Site 1-7	2,123	0.932	1.36	178.6	210.8	32.2	4.2
Site 1-8T	1,705	0.976	1.35	167.3	209.6	42.3	3.2
Site 1-8C	2,123	0.932	1.36	144.7	211.6	66.9	2.0
Site 1-9	2,312	0.953	1.34	177.4	209.2	31.8	4.2
North	1,985	0.902	1.47	188	216.0	28.0	5.3
South	1,436	0.972	1.38	170.8	207.2	36.4	3.8

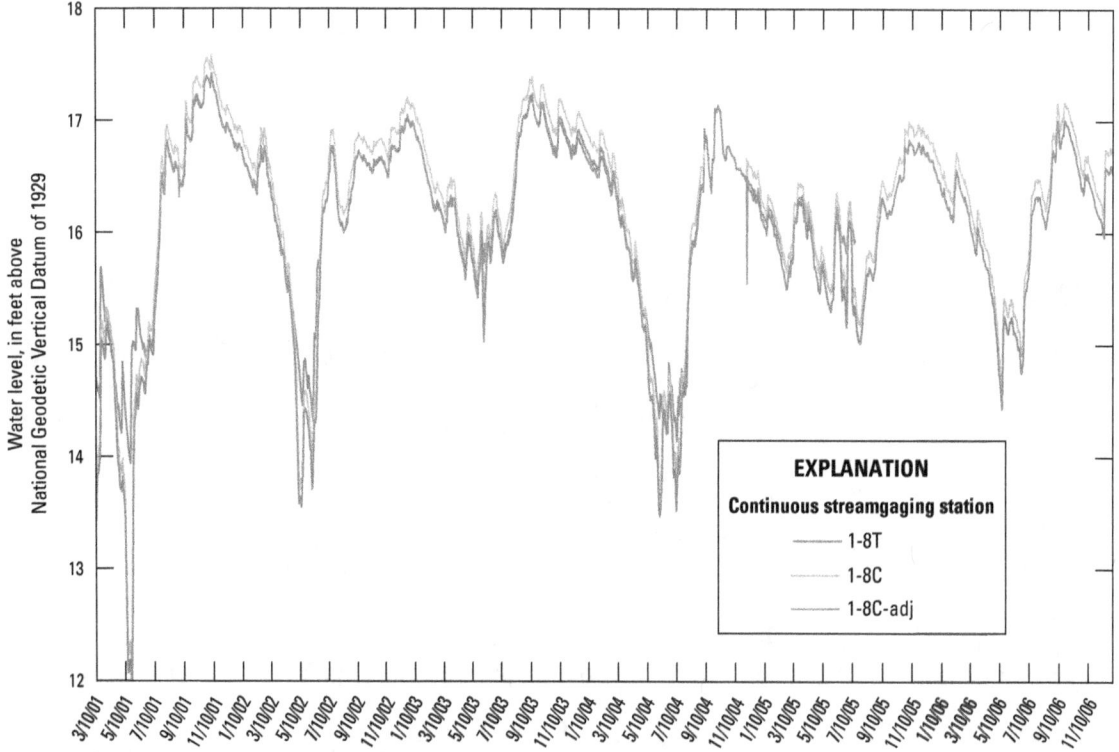

Figure 20. Water levels at sites 1-8T and 1-8C, and a 0.16-foot adjustment to water level at site 1-8C, Arthur R. Marshall Loxahatchee National Wildlife Refuge, Florida, March 2001 to December 2006. See figure 6 for site locations.

Specific Conductance and Total Phosphorus Models

A two-step modeling approach was used to simulate specific conductance and total phosphorus at the XYZ and LOX sampling sites. The specific conductance and total phosphorus process models use water-level inputs, either historical or from the water-level models, and specific conductance and total phosphorus inputs from control structures (fig. 13). The approach uses output from the first SIANN model as input to the second SIANN model. The first submodel (SC_{static} SIANN and TP_{static} SIANN, fig. 13) for each of the models uses only static variable input of location (X and Y coordinates) of the sampling site to predict either specific conductance or total phosphorus. The static models predict a baseline specific conductance or total phosphorus that varies by location but not time. Although the static models are not able to predict the dynamic variability of the specific conductance or total phosphorus, the models are able to discriminate general site-to-site differences on the basis of sampling site location. The baseline is similar to a historical average, but the SIANN automatically spatially interpolates to predict baseline values at unmonitored locations without using a post-processing scheme, such as kriging. The measured data with the specific conductance (25 sampling sites of the XYZ and LOX network) and total phosphorus (14 sampling sites of the LOX network) baseline predictions are shown in figures 21 and 22, respectively, and model performance statistics are listed in table 10. As with the gage height error correction SIANN model, the specific conductance and total phosphorus models used stacked datasets, and the model results are shown with the sampling sites beside one another.

To predict the dynamic components of the specific conductance and total phosphorus signals, the baseline predictions were subtracted from the measured data to compute residual errors from the static SIANN models, ε_{SC} and ε_{TP} (ε_{SC} SIANN and ε_{TP} SIANN, fig. 13). The residual error time series from the static SIANN models (ε_{SC} and ε_{TP}, respectively) are the dynamic components of the specific conductance and total phosphorus signals. The ε_{SC} and ε_{TP} time series were then modeled with SIANNs, such that the sum of the predicted baselines and errors yield predictions of specific conductance and total phosphorus.

Many configurations of inputs for the SIANN models were considered. Itemized below are comments and observations made from evaluating many ANN configurations. The evaluations were made difficult by the sparseness (table 2) and lack of coincidence in measurement of the specific conductance and total phosphorus data from the control structures and the XYZ and LOX sites.

- The specific conductance and total phosphorus data from the control structures were linearly interpolated up to 90 days. The variable name includes "I90" to indicate the 90-day interpolation. The interpolation was necessary in order to use control structure data for input water-quality boundary conditions (S39 $SC_{components}$ and S6 $TP_{components}$, fig. 13); however, using a window size that is relatively large compared to sampling frequency to interpolate presumably spiky signals decreases their signal-to-noise ratio and reliability as predictors.

- Missing site 1-8C water-level values were synthesized by an ANN using water-level inputs calculated from sites having fewer missing values. These filled values in the time series increased the number of site 1-8C values from 3,838 to 3,926. While the increase is small, when missing values are scattered throughout the signal, the number of calculable window averages decreases with increasing window size. (The filled parameter is called F_GH_1-8C, appendix 1.)

Table 10.   Model performance statistics for the static and dynamic specific conductance and total phosphorus models.

[R^2, coefficient of determination; RMSE, root mean square error; —, not applicable]

Model	Training dataset count	Testing dataset count	R^2 (training/testing)	RMSE[a] (training/testing)
Models—Static				
Specific conductance	2,185	0	0.72/0	174/0
Total phosphorus	637	706	0.0185/0.0471	0.0061/0.0047
Models—Dynamic				
Specific conductance	1,470	682	0.522/0.428	119/136
Total phosphorus	1,032	255	0.464/0.601	0.00318/0.00305
Final prediction[b] (sum of static and dynamic model predictions)				
Specific conductance	—	—	0.822	—
Total phosphorus	—	—	0.509	—

[a] Units for RMSE are microsiemens per centimeter for specific conductance and milligrams per liter for total phosphorus.

[b] Statistic computed using all measured and predicted data.

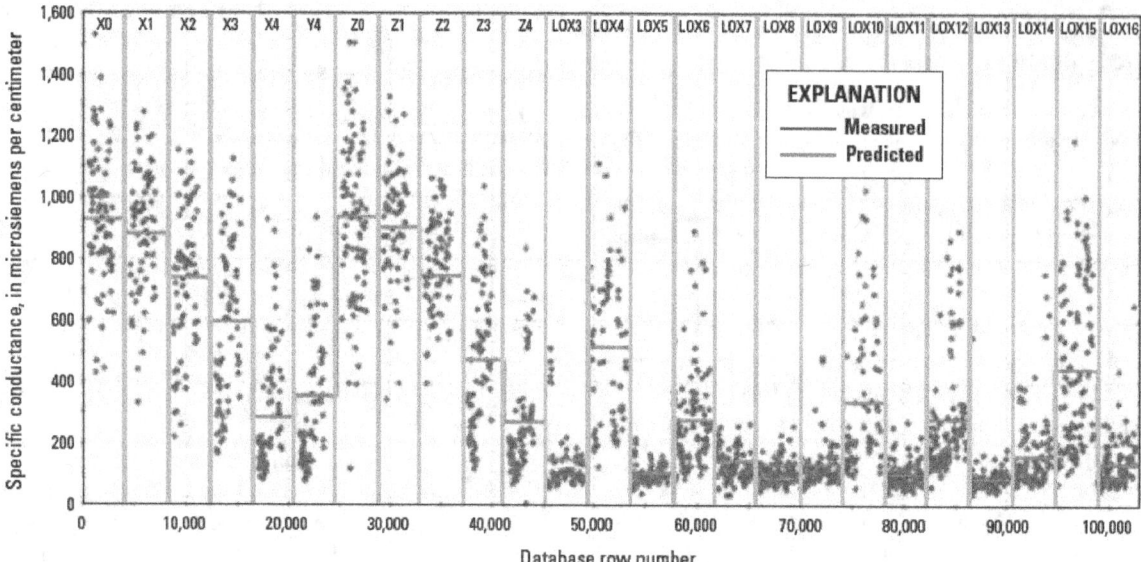

Figure 21. Measured and predicted specific conductance from the static SIANN model for XYZ and EVPA networks, Arthur R. Marshall Loxahatchee National Wildlife Refuge, Florida. Data from January 11, 1995, to December 14, 2004, were used to develop the models. See figure 7 for locations.

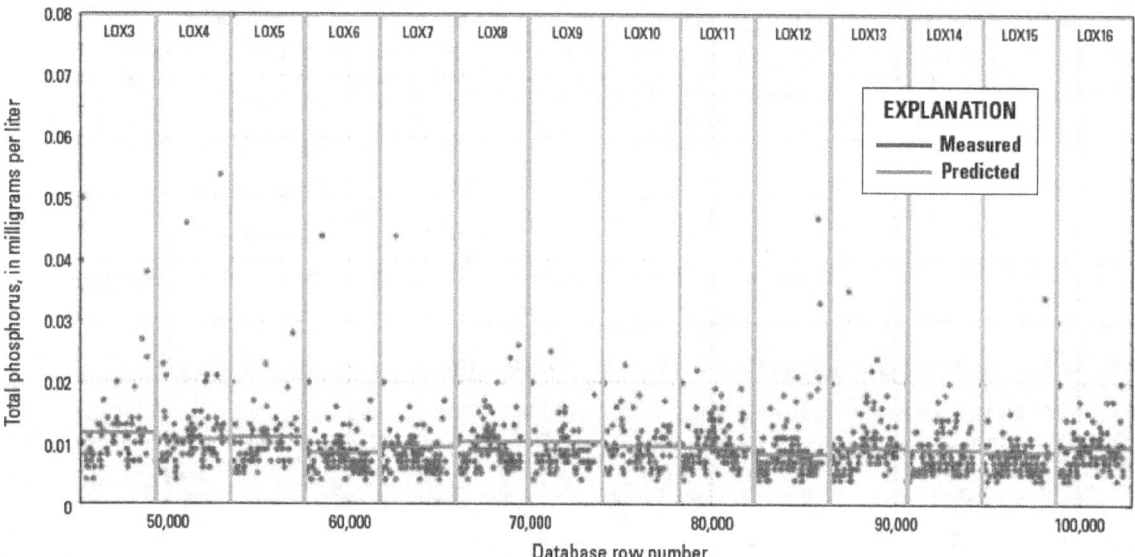

Figure 22. Measured and predicted total phosphorus concentration from the static SIANN models for the EVPA network, Arthur R. Marshall Loxahatchee National Wildlife Refuge, Florida. Data from January 11, 1995, to December 14, 2004, were used to develop the models. See figure 7 for locations.

Modeling Specific Conductance Residual Error (ε_{SC})

The approach for modeling the dynamic specific conductance signal is similar to the approach used for modeling the error of the linear regression water-level models. The rainfall (RAIN) and evapotranspiration (ET) time series were summed at each time step, and the combined variable was named RAIN-ET-COMB. The water levels were normalized by using site 1-8T as a standard, and the daily water levels for the other sites (site 1-7, site 1-8C, site 1-9, north, and south) were subtracted from the water level for site 1-8T. Normalized water-level variable names are designated with the prefix "N_." Moving window averages of 3, 9, 30, 90, and 180 days were calculated for RAIN-ET-COMB, water level at site 1-8T, the normalized water-level parameters, and the 90-day interpolated S-39 control structure specific conductance. For example, RAIN-ET-COMB_A3 is the 3-day moving window average of the combined rainfall and evapotranspiration parameter, RAIN-ET-COMB. Differences between each moving window average and the next larger window-sized moving window average were calculated for each parameter. For example, RAIN-ET-COMB_D3 is the difference between the 3-day (RAIN-ET-COMB_A3) and 9-day (RAIN-ET-COMB_A9) moving window average for the combined rainfall and evapotranspiration parameter. No differences were calculated for the 180-day moving window averages. The following inputs were used in the ε_{SC} SIANN model:

- X, Y coordinates of the XYZ and LOX specific conductance monitoring sites
- RAIN-ET-COMB_D30, RAIN-ET-COMB_D90, RAIN-ET-COMB_A180
- N_GH_1-7_D10
- GH_1-8T_D3, water level_1-8T_D10, GH_1-8T_D30, GH_1-8T_A90
- N_F_GH_1-8C_D3, N_F_GH_1-8C_D9, N_F_GH_1-8C_D30
- S39-specific conductance_I90_A30

The SIANN was trained using approximately 70 percent of the available data, which were randomly selected, with the balance being set aside to test the prediction accuracy of the submodel. The SIANN's predictions of ε_{SC} are shown in figure 23, and model performance statistics are listed in table 10. The final predictions of specific conductance were calculated by summing the output values from the static and SIANN models (fig. 24).

Modeling Total Phosphorus Residual Error (ε_{TP})

Input variables were computed for the ε_{TP} SIANN model as were done for the ε_{SC} SIANN models with the following changes based on higher correlation of input variables to total phosphorus. The water level at site 1-8C instead of site 1-8T was used as the standard to normalize the water levels. The 90-day interpolated control structure input data were from the S6 control structure instead of the S-39 control structure. The following inputs were used in the ε_{SC} SIANN model:

- X, Y=UTM coordinates of the XYZ and LOX specific conductance monitoring sites
- RAIN-ET-COMB_D3, RAIN-ET-COMB_D9, RAIN-ET-COMB_D30, RAIN-ET-COMB_A90
- N_GH_1-7_D3, N_GH_1-7_D9, N_GH_1-7_D30, N_GH_1-7_A90
- N_GH_1-9_D9, N_GH_1-9_D30, N_GH_1-9_A90
- S6-TP_I90_D90, S6-TP_I90_A180

The ε_{TP} SIANN was trained using approximately 80 percent of the available data, which were randomly selected, with the balance being set aside to test the prediction accuracy of the submodel. The SIANN's predictions of ε_{TP} are shown in figure 25. The final predictions of specific conductance were calculated by summing the output values from the static and ε_{TP}-prediction SIANN models (fig. 26), and model performance statistics are listed in table 10.

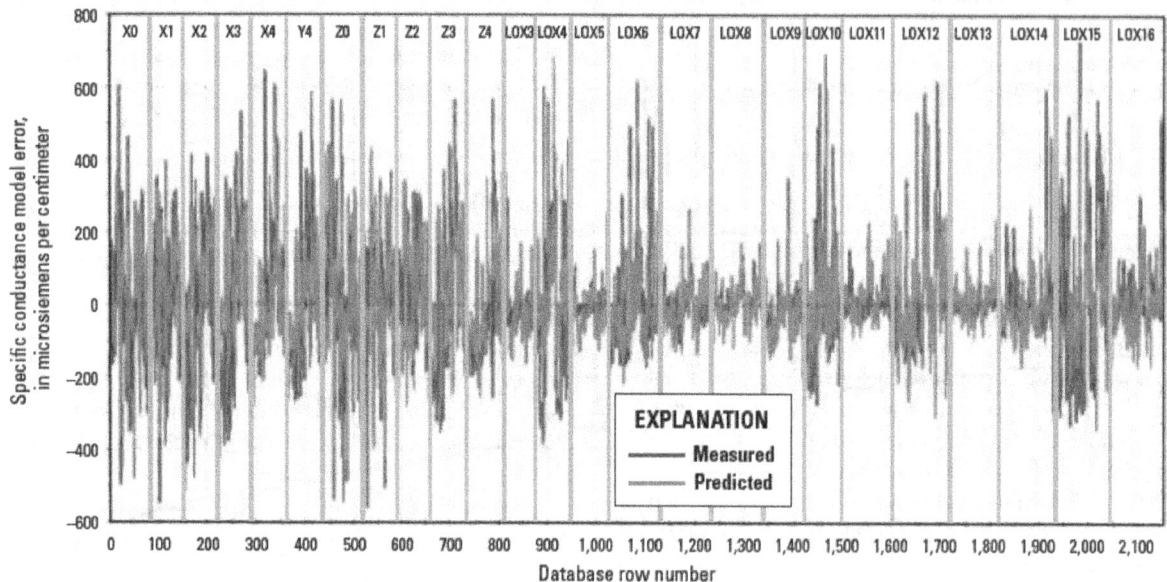

Figure 23.   Measured and predicted specific conductance model error for XYZ and EVPA networks, Arthur R. Marshall Loxahatchee National Wildlife Refuge, Florida. Data from January 11, 1995, to December 14, 2004, were used to develop the models. See figure 7 for locations.

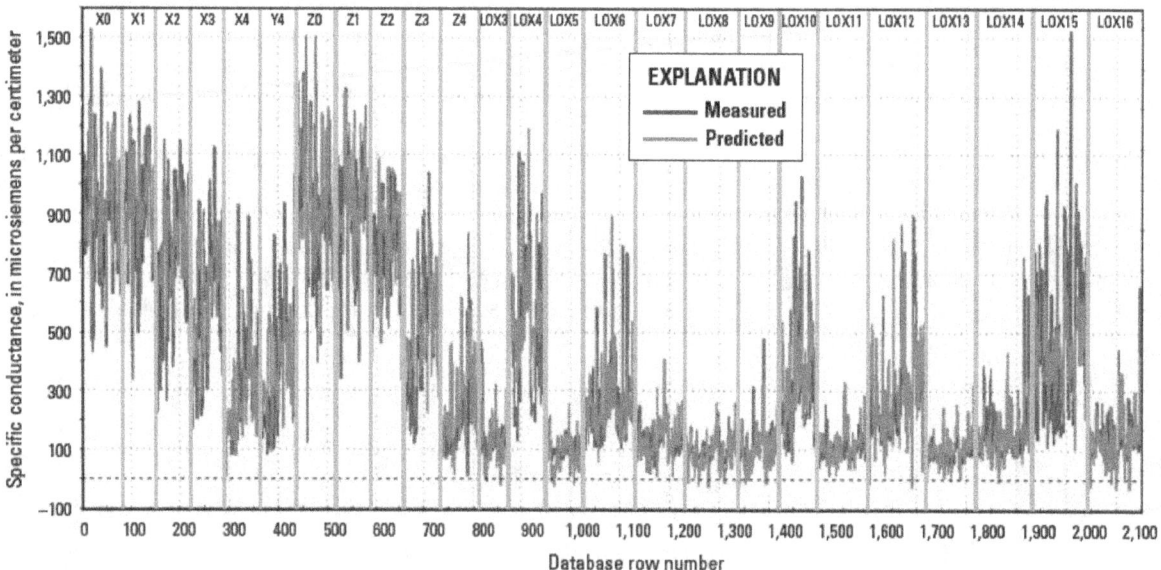

Figure 24.   Measured and predicted specific conductance for XYZ and EVPA networks, Arthur R. Marshall Loxahatchee National Wildlife Refuge, Florida. Data from January 11, 1995, to December 14, 2004, were used to develop the models. See figure 7 for locations.

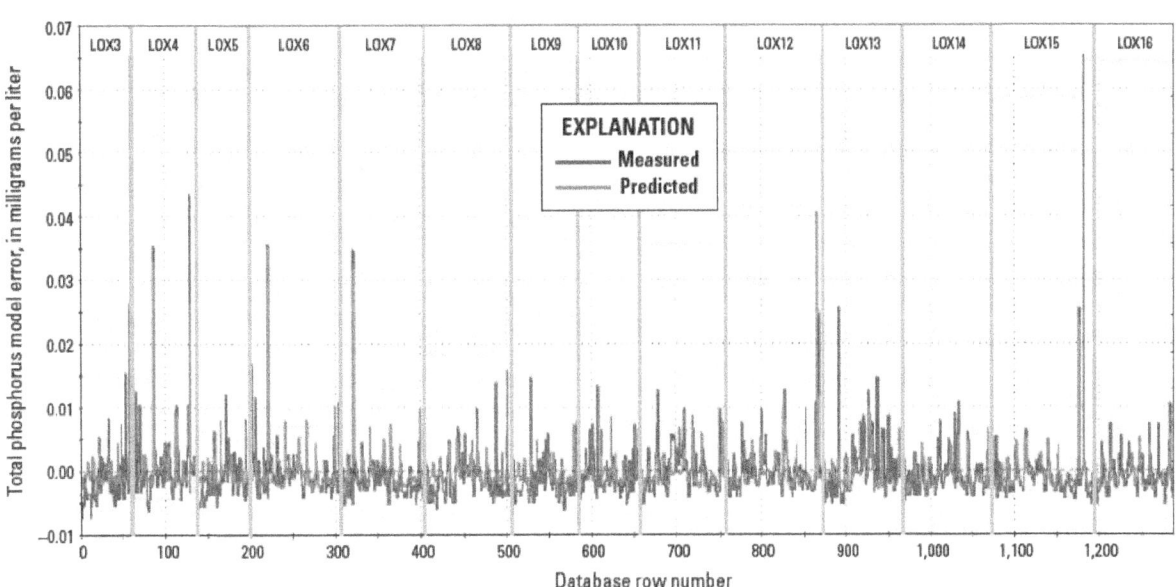

Figure 25. Measured and predicted total phosphorus model error for the EVPA network, Arthur R. Marshall Loxahatchee National Wildlife Refuge, Florida. Data from January 11, 1995, to December 14, 2004, were used to develop the models. See figure 7 for locations.

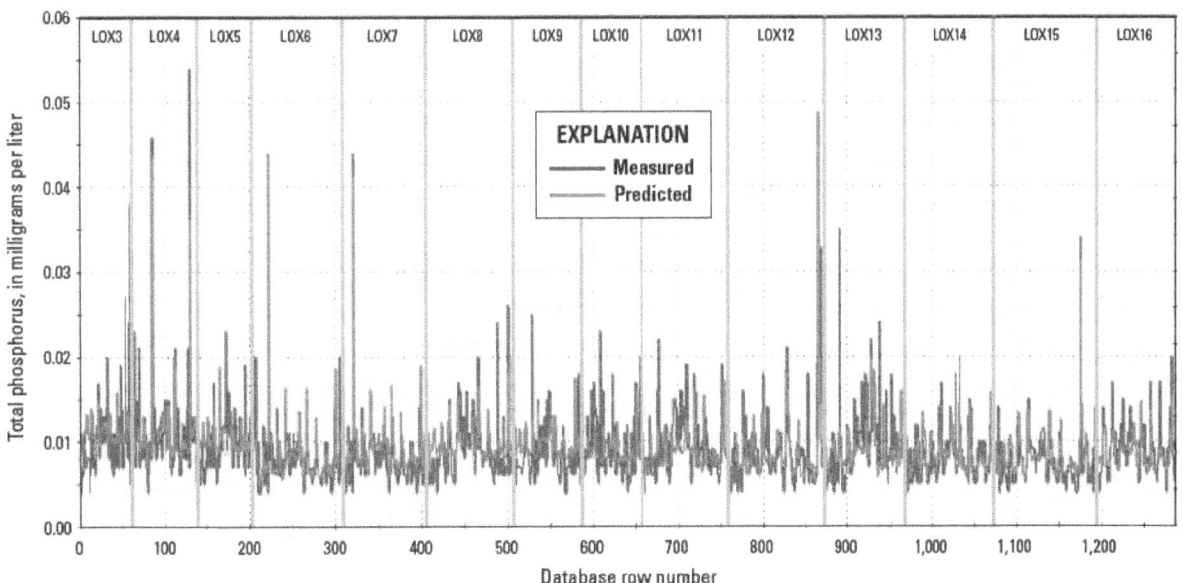

Figure 26. Measured and predicted total phosphorus for the EVPA network, Arthur R. Marshall Loxahatchee National Wildlife Refuge, Florida. Data from January 11, 1995, to December 14, 2004, were used to develop the models. See figure 7 for locations.

Analysis of Specific Conductance and Total Phosphorus Trends Using the Spatially Interpolating Artificial Neural Network Models

The long-term specific conductance and total phosphorus trends can be evaluated using SIANN models that use only inputs of sampling site location (X and Y) and time, the latter represented by an integer counter. This result would be similar to fitting a time-series record with a least-square linear fit and evaluating the trend of the data by the slope of the regression line. Training and testing datasets were selected by a zone-averaging filter that segments the input vector space into partitions of equal size and then selects a user-defined number of vectors from each partition to be used for model training. This ensures that the training data represent the breadth of behaviors manifest in the full dataset, while at the same time balances the prevalence of more and less common behaviors in the training data. The testing data includes the full dataset. The specific conductance SIANN model predictions at the XYZ and LOX sites are shown in figure 27, and the model performance statistics are listed in table 11. Like the other datasets used in the development of the SIANN models, data from the sites are shown with the sampling sites beside one another. The period modeled was from January 11, 1995, to December 14, 2004. The long-term trends at the majority of sites show increasing specific conductance.

The total phosphorus SIANN model for trend analysis used the same inputs of location and time as the specific conductance SIANN model. The training and testing datasets were selected randomly with approximately 80 percent of the data used for training. The total phosphorus SIANN model predictions at the XYZ and LOX sites are shown in figure 28,

and the model performance statistics are listed in table 11. Data from the sites are shown with the sampling sites beside one another. The period modeled was from January 11, 1995, to December 14, 2004. Unlike the linear increase seen at the majority of the specific conductance sites, the total phosphorus predictions show an oscillatory response with a peak concentration approximately halfway through the simulation period and an increasing trend at the end of the simulation period.

Color gradient maps of specific conductance and total phosphorus were created using the SIANN model predictions for dates corresponding to the beginning, midpoint, and end of the modeled period, or January 11, 1995, December 28, 1999, and December 14, 2004, respectively. In figure 29, red triangles and magenta squares mark the XYZ and LOX sampling sites, respectively. The magenta boundaries mark the convex hull (or region of model interpolation) of the X and Y coordinates of the sites included in each SIANN model. Simulations outside the convex hulls are model extrapolations. The specific conductance maps for the successive dates show an increasing trend throughout the Refuge that also is seen in the specific conductance simulations at the majority of the sampling sites (fig. 27). The figure indicates that there may be mixing of the higher conductance canal water with lower conductance marsh water. The maps of total phosphorus show variability in both concentrations and prevailing gradient directions. The total phosphorus simulations (fig. 28) also show the temporal variability and a similarity in the nonlinear trends between the sampling sites. The variability may be caused by changes in annual loading to the system, effectiveness of the stormwater-treatment areas, interannual hydrologic variability of the magnitude of wet and dry seasons, or storm activity, such as hurricanes.

Table 11.   Model performance statistics for the specific conductance and total phosphorus models used for trend analysis.

[R^2, coefficient of determination; RMSE, root mean square error]

Model	Training dataset count	Testing dataset count	R^2 (training/testing)	RMSE[a] (training/testing)
Specific conductance	210	2,212	0.80/0.69	109/187
Total phosphorus	1,054	273	0.078/0.055	0.0035/0.0033

[a] Units for RMSE are microsiemens per centimeter for specific conductance and milligrams per liter for total phosphorus.

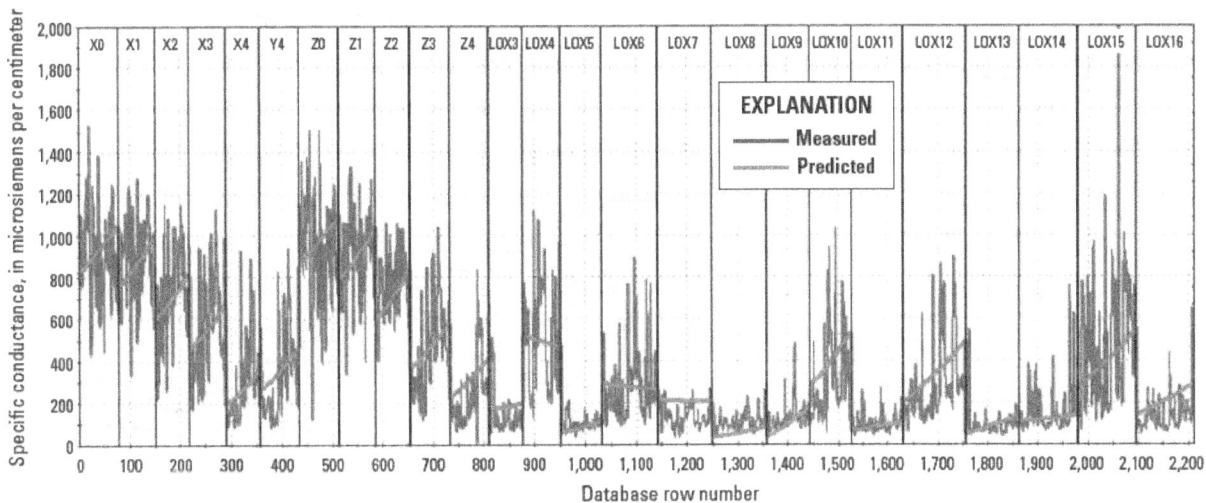

Figure 27. Measured and predicted specific conductance to evaluate trends at XYZ and EVPA networks, Arthur R. Marshall Loxahatchee National Wildlife Refuge, Florida. Simulations were made by a SIANN using only X, Y, and time as inputs. Data from January 11, 1995, to December 14, 2004, were used to develop the models. See figure 7 for locations.

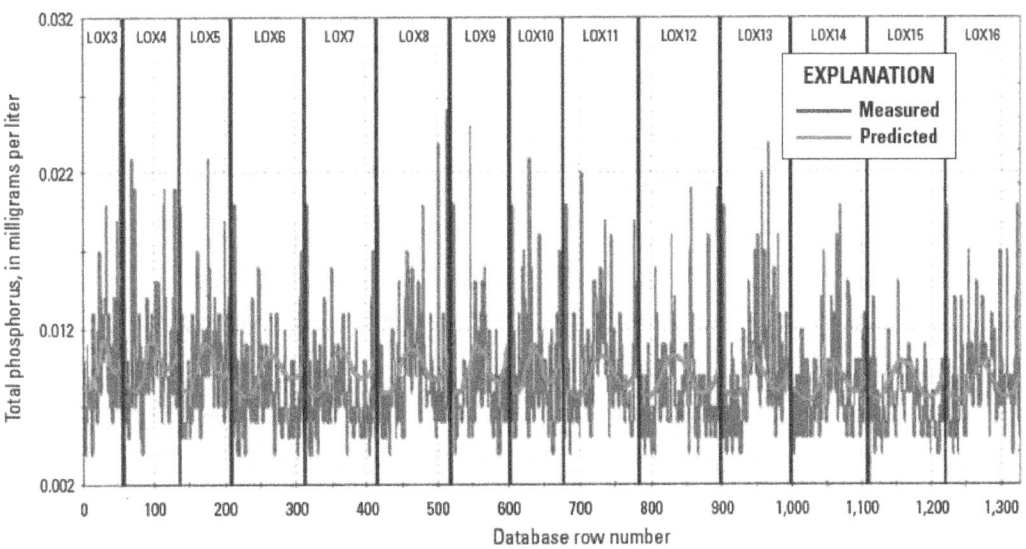

Figure 28. Measured and predicted total phosphorus to evaluate trends at EVPA networks, Arthur R. Marshall Loxahatchee National Wildlife Refuge, Florida. Simulations were made by a SIANN using only X, Y, and time as inputs. Data from January 11, 1995, to December 14, 2004, were used to develop the models. See figure 7 for locations.

Figure 29. Color gradient maps of specific conductance and total phosphorus as predicted by SIANNs for the Arthur R. Marshall Loxahatchee National Wildlife Refuge, Florida. *(A)* January 11, 1995; *(B)* December 28, 1999; *(C)* December 14, 2004.

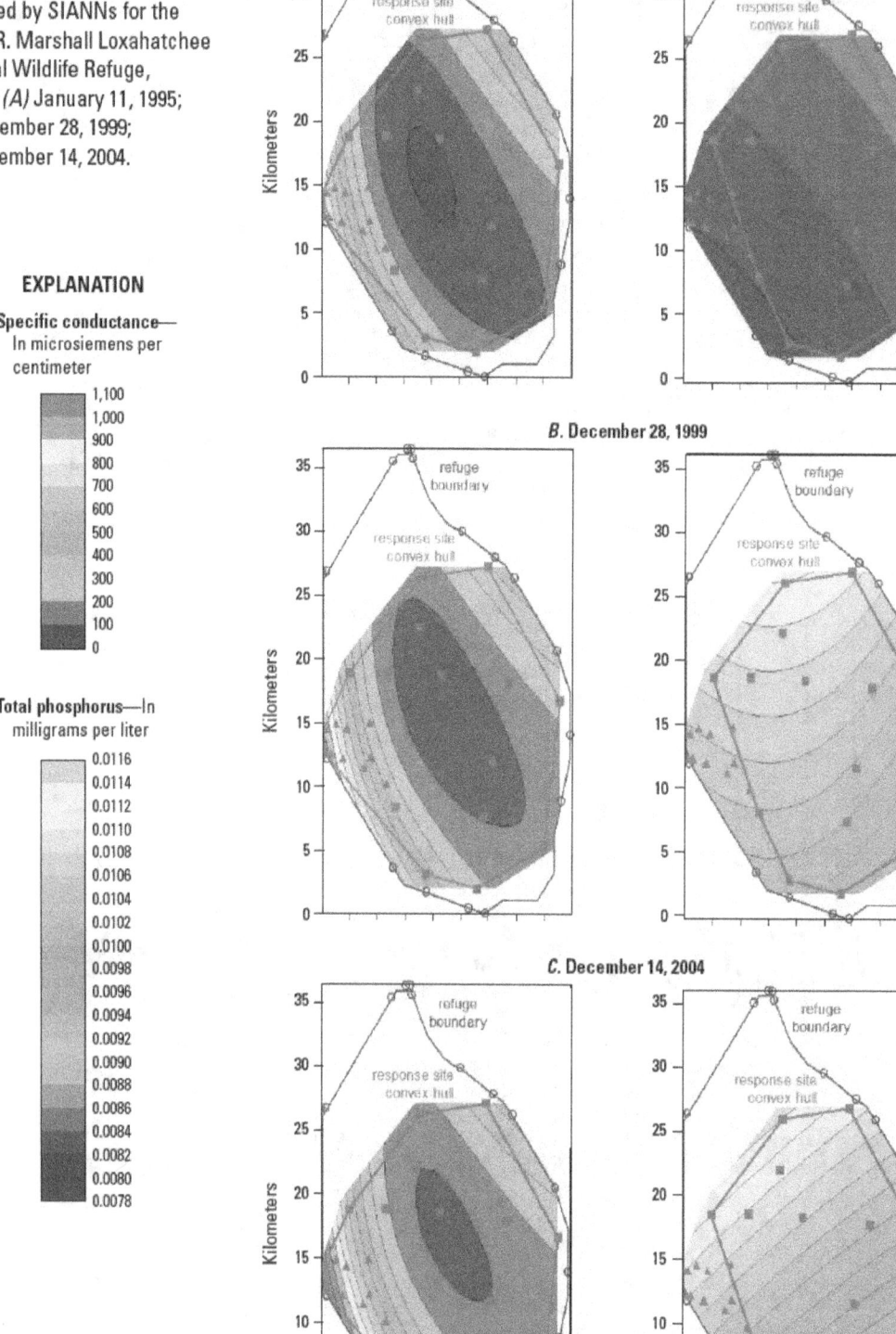

EXPLANATION

Specific conductance—
In microsiemens per centimeter

1,100
1,000
900
800
700
600
500
400
300
200
100
0

Total phosphorus—In milligrams per liter

0.0116
0.0114
0.0112
0.0110
0.0108
0.0106
0.0104
0.0102
0.0100
0.0098
0.0096
0.0094
0.0092
0.0090
0.0088
0.0086
0.0084
0.0082
0.0080
0.0078

Development of the Decision Support System

Resource managers and stakeholders face difficult challenges when managing interactions between natural and manmade systems. Complex mechanistic models based on first principles physical equations are often developed and operated by scientists at considerable costs to evaluate options for using a resource while minimizing harm. However, varying technical abilities and financial constraints among different stakeholders effectively restrict access to relevant scientific knowledge and tools. Decision support system technology can help meet the need to provide equal access to the knowledge and tools required for informed decision making. Even though the collective interests and computer skills within the community of managers, scientists, and other stakeholders are quite varied, equal access to the scientific information is needed in order to make the best possible decisions. Dutta and others (1997) define DSSs as "systems helping decision-makers to solve various semi-structured and unstructured problems involving multiple attributes, objectives, and goals... Historically, the majority of DSSs have been either computer implementations of mathematical models or extensions of database systems and traditional management information systems." While there appears to be no strict criteria that distinguish a DSS from other types of programs, Dutta and others (1997) suggest that artificial intelligence (AI) is a characteristic of more advanced DSSs: "With the help of AI techniques DSSs have incorporated the heuristic models of decision makers and provided increasingly richer support for decision making. Artificial intelligence systems also have benefited from DSS research as they have scaled down their goal from replacing to supporting decision makers."

The authors of this report have previously developed three DSSs in South Carolina and Georgia to evaluate (1) wastewater discharges and dissolved-oxygen concentration in the Beaufort River estuary (Conrads and others, 2003; Roehl and others, 2006b); (2) salinity effects on freshwater tidal wetland and a proposed deepening of the Savannah Harbor (Conrads and others, 2006); and (3) the effect of controlled flow releases from reservoirs on the Pee Dee River in North Carolina and on salinity dynamics along the South Carolina coast (Conrads and Roehl, 2007). These DSSs are spreadsheet applications that provide predictive models with real-time databases for ANN model simulation, graphical user interfaces, and displays of results. Additional features include optimizers, integrations with other models and software tools, and color contouring of simulation output data. These features make the DSSs easily distributable and immediately usable by all resource managers and stakeholders.

The development of a DSS for the Refuge required a number of steps (described previously), including (1) merging all the data into a single comprehensive database; (2) developing water-level, specific conductance, and total phosphorus linear regression and SIANN submodels; and (3) developing a Microsoft Office Excel® application that integrates the new database, submodels, and visualization routines into a single package that is easy to use and disseminate. The user's manual for the installation and operation of the LOXANN DSS is available in appendix 2.

Architecture

The basic architectural elements of the LOXANN DSS are shown in figure 30. The DSS reads and writes files for the various run-time options that can be selected by the user through the system's graphical user interface. A historical database, containing 12 years of hydrologic data, is read into the simulator along with the linear regression and SIANN submodels at the start of a simulation. By using graphical user interface controls, the user can evaluate alternative flow scenarios. The outputs generated by the simulator are written to files for post processing in Microsoft Office Excel® or other analysis software packages. The DSS also provides streaming graphics for each gage during simulations and three-dimensional visualization of the water-level, specific conductance, and total phosphorus response for the Refuge models.

Model Simulation Control, Streaming Graphics, and Three-Dimensional Visualization Program

The simulator in the LOXANN DSS integrates the historical database with the six linear regression models and five SIANN models. The date/time controls on the user control panel (fig. 31) are used to adjust start and end dates and parameters (water level, specific conductance, and (or) total phosphorus) for a simulation. The simulator allows the user to run "what-if" simulations by varying the control-structure flows from their historical values. There are two types of inputs to a model: (1) controllable variables, such as the control-structure flows, and (2) uncontrollable state variables, such as rainfall and evapotranspiration. To evaluate alternative courses of action, the controllable inputs can be manually manipulated by the user while the uncontrollable and constantly changing variables representing rainfall and

evapotranspiration are set to their historical values. The user has three simulation input variable options:

- percentage of historical control-structure flow to the system,

- user-defined control-structure flow to a constant value, or

- user-defined flow hydrograph for one or more control structures.

Explanations of how to use each of the options in the LOXANN DSS can be found in the user's manual in appendix 2.

For each water-level gage or sampling site, a worksheet displays streaming graphics while a simulation is running for any three simulated variables selected by the user (fig. 32). The graphs display the historical measured data, simulated historical conditions (to show model accuracy), and the simulated output using control-structure flow set by the user using the graphical user interface controls or an input file. A table in the worksheet shows the input data to the model, including rainfall, evapotranspiration, and aggregated control-structure flows.

The three-dimensional visualization (3DVis) worksheet in the LOXANN DSS provides graphical profiles of water level, specific conductance, and total phosphorus for the region of the Refuge simulated by the models (fig. 33). The 3DVis worksheet is designed to visualize and animate periods of special interest. Data and the controls for operating the 3DVis worksheet are on the left side of the 3DVis worksheet. The data are a subset of those in the "Control" worksheet (appendix 2) and are provided for reference while using the 3DVis worksheet. Surfaces of gage height, specific conductance, and total phosphorus are shown in figure 33. The surface on the left shows the profile representing the actual historical data (when available), and the surface on the right shows the surface predicted by the models using the user-specified flow conditions.

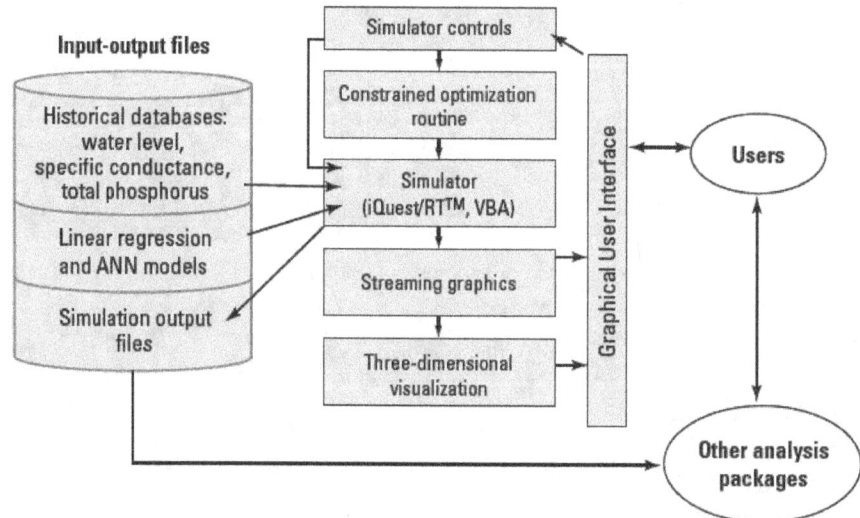

Figure 30. Architecture of the LOXahatchee Artificial Neural Network (LOXANN) decision support system.

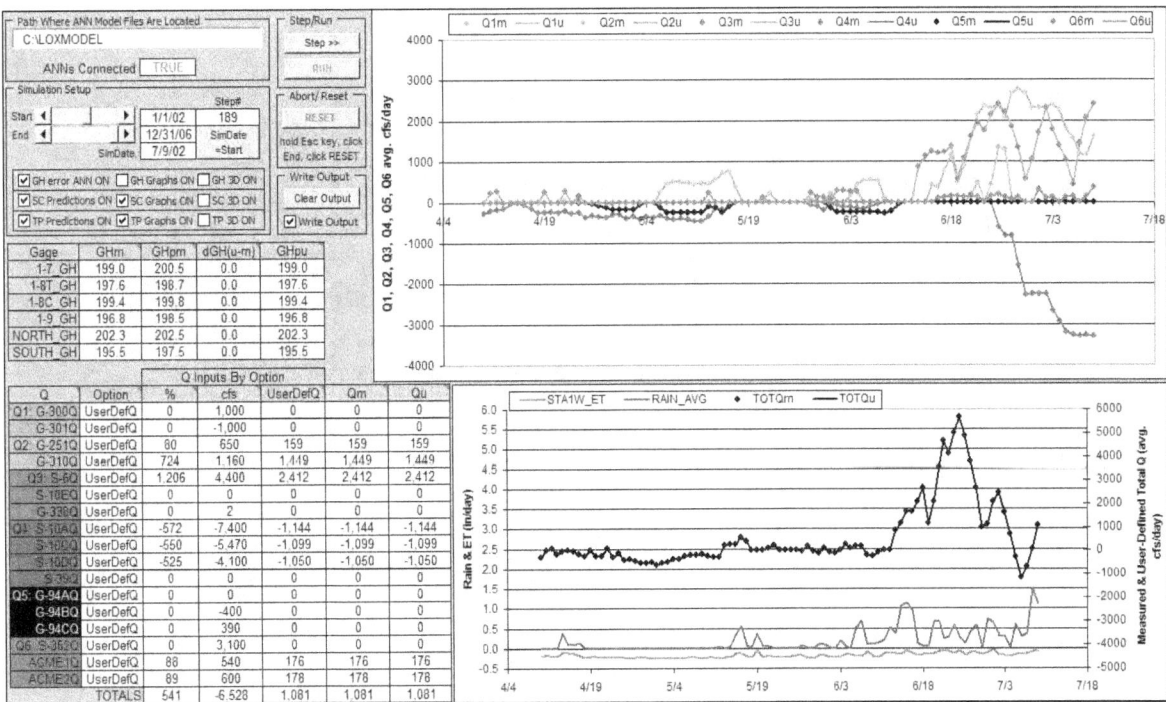

Figure 31. Model simulator controls used to set parameters and run a simulation in the LOXANN decision support system.

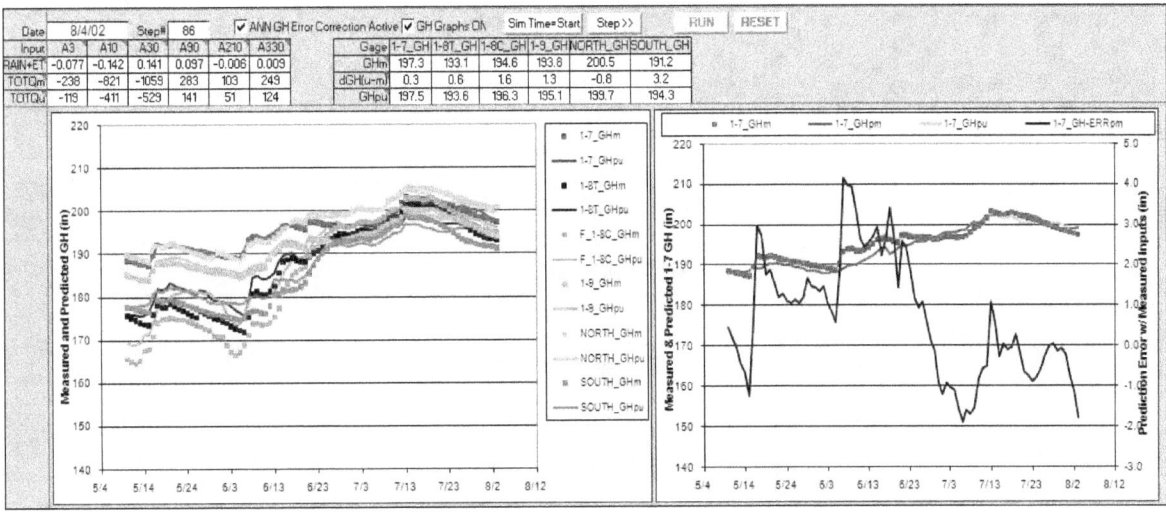

Figure 32. Streaming graphics displayed during simulation in the LOXANN decision support system.

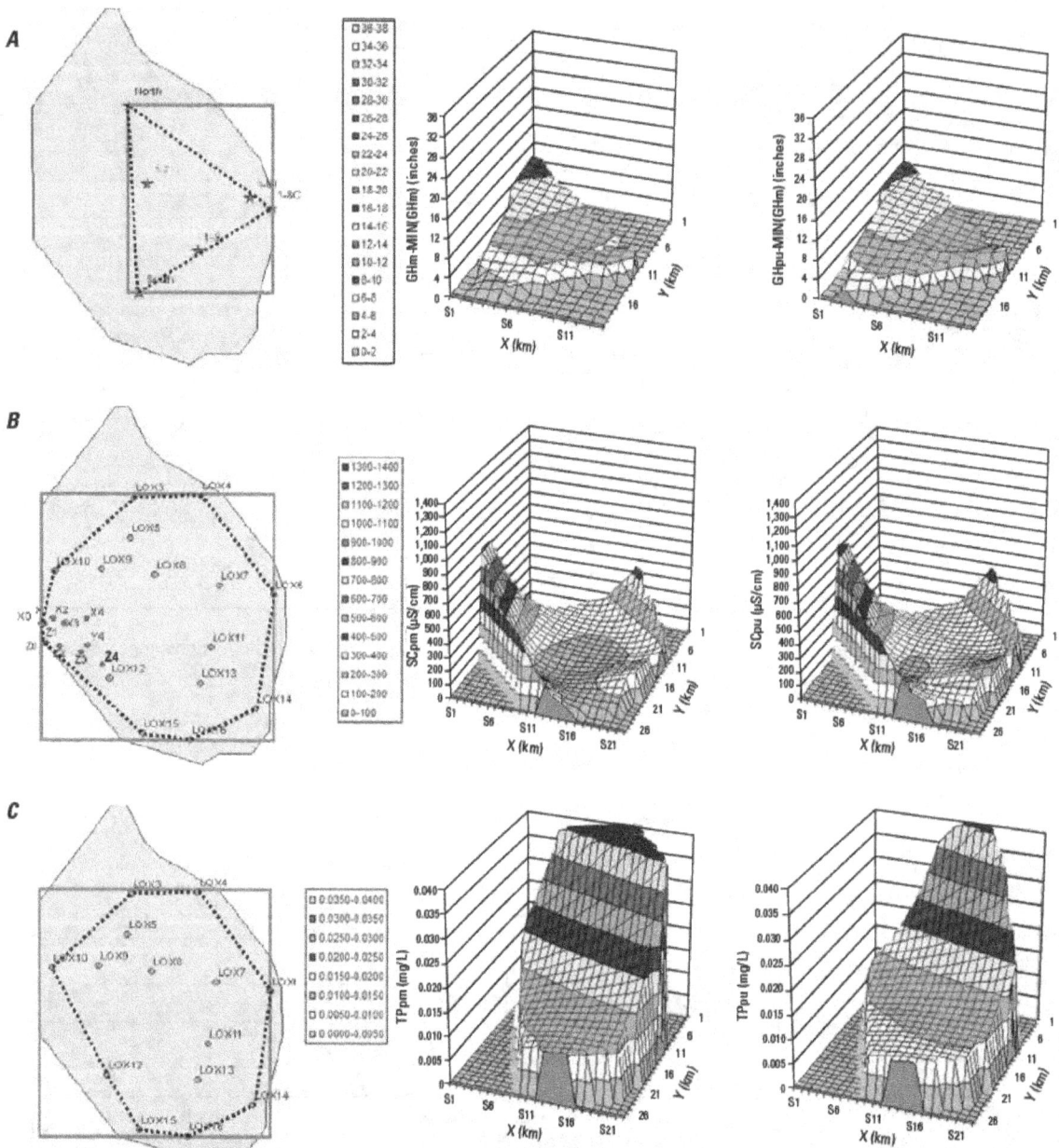

Figure 33.   Three-dimensional surfaces of *(A)* water levels, *(B)* specific conductance, and *(C)* total phosphorus, Arthur R. Marshall Loxahatchee National Wildlife Refuge, Florida. Maps on the left show the region of the particular model interpolation. Surfaces on the left represent actual conditions and surfaces on the right represent a user-defined scenario. Values in the cells are calculated by linear interpolation (water levels) or spatially interpolating artificial neural network models.

Application of the LOXANN Decision Support System

The development of the linear regression and SIANN models and the DSS application for the Refuge provides resource managers with a tool to evaluate water level, specific conductance, and total phosphorus dynamics in the areas of the Refuge. The LOXANN DSS allows users to simulate various control structure flow conditions and analyze the water-level, specific conductance, and total phosphorus response as an aid to understanding water-quantity and water- quality dynamics in the Refuge. The increase in specific conductance and total phosphorus in the marsh is a result of canal water intruding into the marsh. This increase occurs when water levels are higher in the canal than the water level in the marsh and higher nutrient concentration of canal water mixes with marsh water near the canals. The greater the water-level gradient between the canal and the marsh, the further the high nutrient concentration water will enter into the marsh. Large increases in the water-level gradient could have the negative effect of increasing flows leaving the marsh and drying out the wetland.

In the LOXANN DSS, the user is able to set control-structure flows as a constant flow, a percentage of historical flow, or as a user-defined hydrograph. These settings also can be set in combinations. For example, some structures can be set to a constant flow, while others are set to a percentage of historical flow, and others to a user-defined flow. The following section describes applications of the LOXANN-DSS to two hydrologic scenarios. The results from these scenarios

are intended to demonstrate the utility of the LOXANN DSS and are not intended to be interpreted as potential hydraulic operations or a regulatory application of the DSS.

Percentage of Historical Flow

One user-specified option is to set the control-structure flows at a percentage of the historical flow. To evaluate the change to the slope between the canal (site 1-8C) and the marsh (site 1-7), the flow for the aggregated Q4 flows (structures S-39, S-10A, S-10C, and S-10D) was set to 140 percent of the historical flows for the 6-year period of May 1, 2000, to April 30, 2006. The Q4 flows are negative, or out of the Refuge, so an increase in the flows indicates an increase in the flows leaving the Refuge. The slope between sites 1-8C and 1-7 was computed for the simulated actual flow conditions and the user-specified setting of 40-percent increase in the Q4 flows (fig. 34). The increased flow out of the canal decreased the water-level elevation in the canal and reduced the occurrence of negative slopes and potential intrusion conditions for flows into the interior of the marsh as seen for extended periods of time such as September 2001 to April 2002 and September 2003 to April 2004.

Another method for evaluating the model results is to plot the results as a cumulative frequency distribution rather than a time series (fig. 35). The simulated actual conditions show that the negative slopes (of all magnitudes) occur about 40 percent of the time. Increasing the flows out of the four Q4 control structures by 40 percent decreased the percentage of time that negative slopes occurred to less than 10 percent of the time.

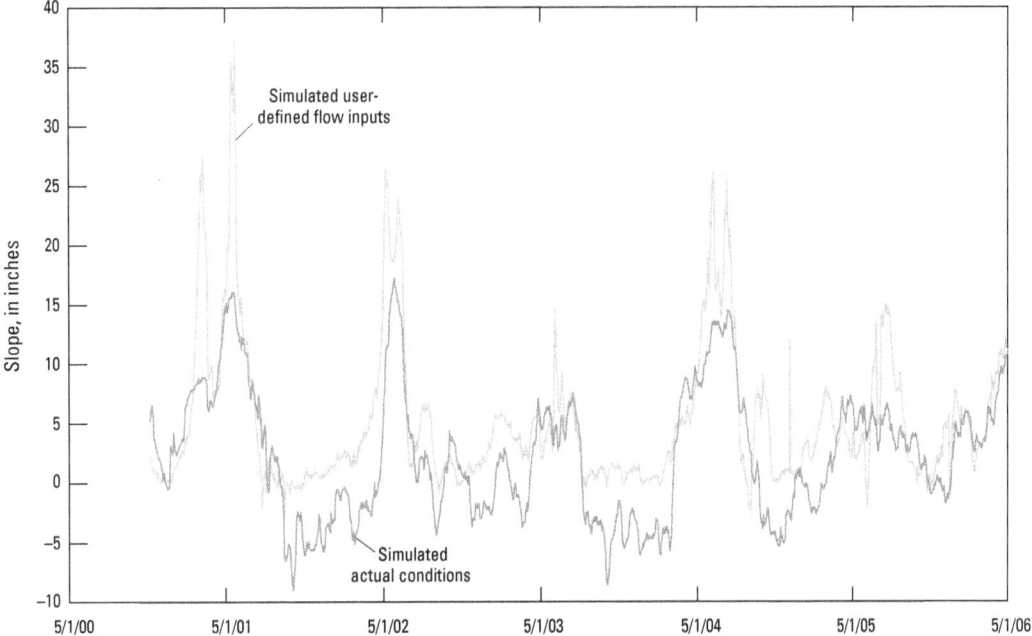

Figure 34.   Simulated actual conditions and a 40-percent increase to the historical flows for aggregated flows of Q4 Arthur R. Marshall Loxahatchee National Wildlife Refuge, Florida May 2000 through April 2006. Gaps in simulations are due to one or more missing inputs to the models. See figure 8 for location.

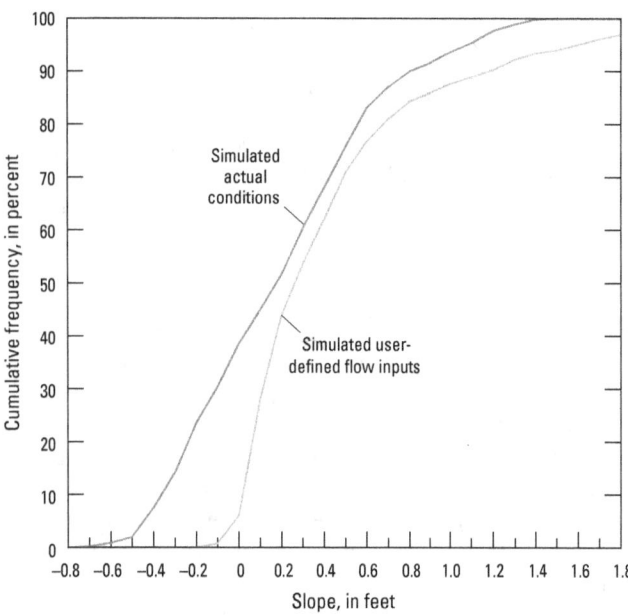

Figure 35. Cumulative frequency of slopes from the canal to marsh for simulated actual conditions and a 40-percent increase to the historical flows for the aggregated Q4 control-structure flow, Arthur R. Marshall Loxahatchee National Wildlife Refuge, Florida. Data generated from a simulation from May 2000 through April 2006. See figure 8 for location.

User-Defined Hydrograph

Another user-specified option is to create a user-defined hydrograph to use for input for one or more of the control structures. With this option, daily hydrographs for the control structure(s) of interest are created outside of the LOXANN DSS. The simulation period is selected and the DSS uses the user-defined hydrographs as inputs for the simulation period. One scenario was simulated using this option. The sum of the inflows and outflows was computed for the 4-year period 2001–2004, and flows into the Refuge were 50-percent greater than flows out of the Refuge (2,080,000 and 812,000 cubic feet per second, respectively; fig. 36). A user-defined hydrograph was computed for the flow structure for Q4 where the outflow from the Refuge equals the weekly average of the inflows to the Refuge delayed by 2 days. Although the user-defined outflow hydrograph does not appear to be substantially different from the measured outflow hydrograph, the total outflow is increased by more than 50 percent to equal the inflow hydrograph. There are periods, such as November 2001 through February 2002, August 2002 through November 2002, and September 2003 through November 2003, where the outflows are noticeably increased from the actual outflows.

Time series and cumulative frequency plots show that increasing the outflow from the Refuge had the effect of reducing the magnitude of the negative slopes and potential for intrusion of canal water into the marsh (figs. 37, 38). Increasing the outflow also had the effect of increasing the positive slopes above 15 inches by up to 20 inches (fig. 37) and decreasing the negative slopes between 0 and 8 inches to 3 inches or less.

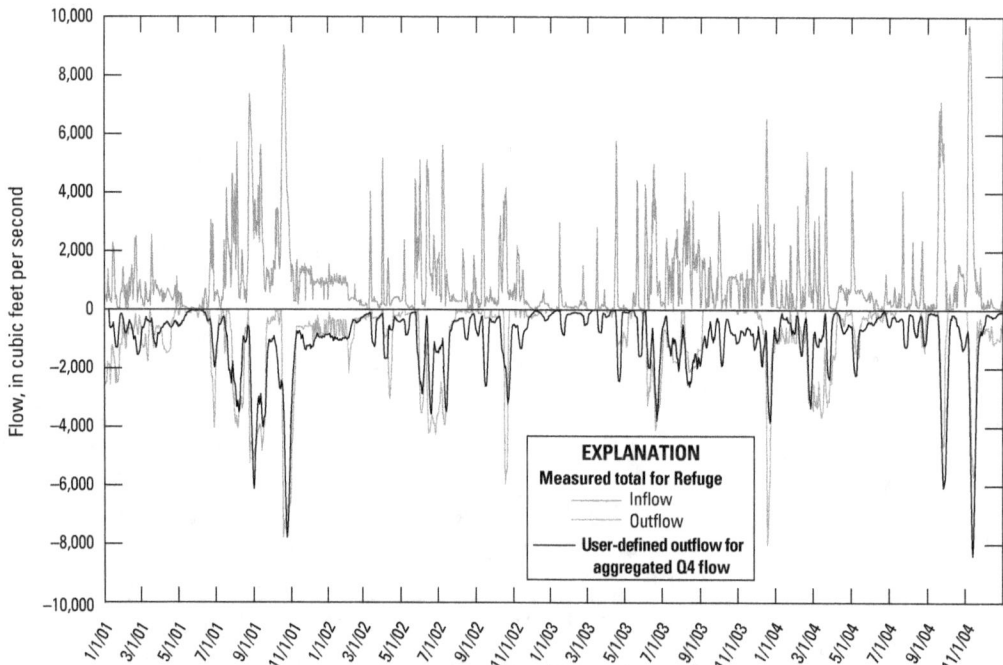

Figure 36. Historical inflow and outflow hydrographs and a user-defined hydrograph for the aggregated Q4 flow, Arthur R. Marshall Loxahatchee National Wildlife Refuge, Florida, January 2001 through December 2004. See figure 8 for location.

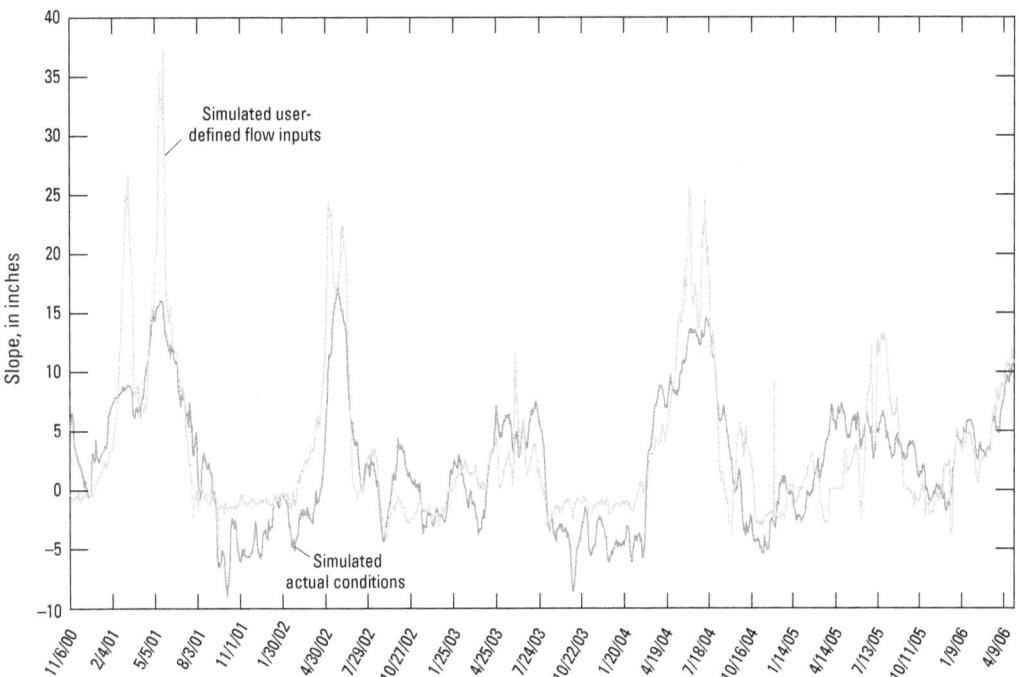

Figure 37. Simulated actual conditions and conditions from a user-defined hydrograph for aggregated flows of Q4, Arthur R. Marshall Loxahatchee National Wildlife Refuge, Florida, January 2001 to April 2006. Gaps in simulations due to one or more missing inputs to the models. See figure 8 for location.

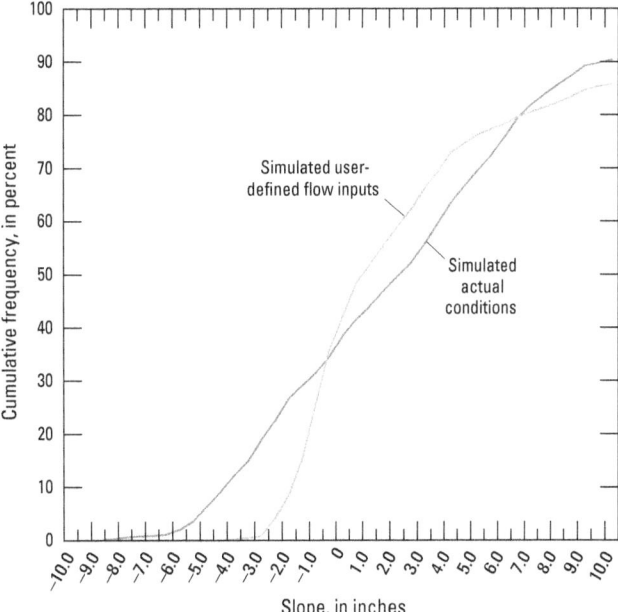

Figure 38. Cumulative frequency of slopes from the canal to marsh for simulated actual conditions and a user-defined hydrograph for the aggregated Q4 control-structure flows, Arthur R. Marshall Loxahatchee National Wildlife Refuge, Florida. Data generated from a simulation from January 2001 through December 2006. See figure 8 for location.

Summary

The Arthur R. Marshall Loxahatchee National Wildlife Refuge (Refuge) is the last of the soft-water ecological systems with low calcium or magnesium ion concentrations in the Everglades. Historically, the ecosystem was driven by precipitation inputs to the system that were low in specific conductance and nutrients. Water levels and water quality in the flow-controlled canals surrounding the Refuge have the potential to alter the critical ecosystem functions of the Refuge marsh because of the transport of water with higher specific conductance and nutrient concentrations.

The U.S. Geological Survey and the U.S. Fish and Wildlife Service realized an opportunity existed to develop an empirical model using data-mining techniques, including artificial neural networks (ANNs), to simulate water level, specific conductance, and total phosphorus in the interior marsh of the Refuge by using the large databases of hydrologic and water-quality data. Hydrologic and water-quality data have been collected in the Refuge for many years. Data characterizing the hydrology of the system—inflows, outflows, precipitation, and water levels—have been collected since the 1950s. Data characterizing the water quality of the system, including specific conductance and total phosphorus, have been collected since the late 1970s. New technologies in environmental monitoring have made it cost effective to acquire tremendous amounts of hydrologic and water-quality data.

Empirical linear regression and ANN models to simulate water level, specific conductance, and total phosphorus were developed using data-mining techniques. Data mining is a powerful tool for converting large databases into information to solve complex problems resulting from large numbers of explanatory variables or poorly understood process physics. For the application of the linear regression and ANN models to the Refuge, data-mining methods were applied to maximize the information content in the raw data. Inputs to the empirical models include time series, or signals, of inflows and outflows from the control structures, precipitation, and evapotranspiration. For a complex hydrologic system like the Refuge, the statistical accuracy of the models and predictive capability are good. The water-level models have coefficient of determination (R^2) values ranging from 0.90 to 0.98. Specific conductance at 25 sites and total phosphorus at 14 sites were modeled using spatially interpolating ANN models. The R^2 for the specific conductance model is 0.82, and the R^2 for the total phosphorus model is 0.51. The accuracy of the models is attributable to the quantity and quality of the available data. The water-level models were developed using daily water-level, flow, rainfall, and evapotranspiration data. The available specific conductance and total phosphorus data were temporally sparse for developing daily models.

The water-level, specific conductance, and total phosphorus models, historical database, model simulation controls, streaming graphics, and model output were integrated into a decision support system (DSS) named the Loxahatchee Artificial Neural Network Model (LOXANN) DSS. The LOXANN DSS allows the user to manipulate the flow inputs to the system. Three options are available to the user in setting the control-structure flows: percentage of historical flow, constant flow, and a user-defined hydrograph. Output from the LOXANN DSS includes tabular time series of predictions of the measured data and predictions of the user-specified conditions. A three-dimensional visualization routine also was developed that displays longitudinal specific conductance conditions. The visualization routine uses predictions at the gaging station or sampling locations and interpolates values among stations. The LOXANN DSS is a spreadsheet application that facilitates the dissemination and utility of the DSS.

Two scenarios were simulated with the LOXANN DSS. One scenario increased the historical flows at the S-39, S-10A, S-10C, and S-10D control structures by 40 percent. The second scenario used a user-defined hydrograph to set the outflow from the Refuge to the weekly average inflow to the Refuge delayed by 2 days. Both scenarios decreased the potential of canal water intruding into the marsh by decreasing the slope of the water level between the canal (site 1-8C) and the marsh (site 1-7).

Acknowledgments

The complexity of this study required interagency cooperation in addition to individual contributions. The authors thank Drs. Mike Waldon and Laura Brandt of the U.S. Fish and Wildlife Service for their coordination of the project and for sharing their technical expertise and knowledge of the system, Dr. Ehab Moselle and his graduate students at the University of Louisiana Lafayette for sharing their compiled historical data, and Dr. Donnato Surratte of the U.S. Fish and Wildlife Service for providing data and technical feedback of interim project technical presentations.

References Cited

Arceneaux, J.C., Meselhe, E.A., and Waldon, M.G., 2007, The Arthur R. Marshall Loxahatchee National Wildlife Refuge water budget and water quality models: Lafayette, University of Louisiana, prepared for the U.S. Fish and Wildlife Service, Department of Interior, by the Institute of Coastal Ecology and Engineering, Report # LOXA-07-004, 172 p.

Conrads, P.A., and Roehl, E.A., 1999, Comparing physics-based and neural network models for predicting salinity, water temperature, and dissolved oxygen concentration in a complex tidally affected river basin: South Carolina Environmental Conference, March 15–19, 1999, Myrtle Beach.

Conrads, P.A., and Roehl, E.A., 2005, Integration of data mining techniques with mechanistic models to determine the impacts of non-point source loading on dissolved oxygen in tidal waters: South Carolina Environmental Conference, March 2005, Myrtle Beach.

Conrads, P.A., and Roehl, E.A., Jr., 2007, Analysis of salinity intrusion in the Waccamaw River and the Atlantic Intracoastal Waterway near Myrtle Beach, South Carolina, 1995–2002: U.S. Geological Survey Scientific Investigations Report 2007–5110, 41 p., 2 apps.

Conrads, P.A., Roehl, E.A., Daamen, R.C., and Kitchens, W.M., 2006, Simulation of water levels and salinity in the rivers and tidal marshes in the vicinity of the Savannah National Wildlife Refuge, Coastal South Carolina and Georgia: U.S. Geological Survey Scientific Investigations Report 2006–5187, 134 p.

Conrads, P.A., Roehl, E.A., and Martello, W.B., 2003, Development of an empirical model of a complex, tidally affected river using artificial neural networks: Water Environment Federation, National TMDL Science and Policy 2003 Specialty Conference, November 2003, Chicago, IL.

Davis, J.H., Jr., 1943, Vegetation map of Southern Florida: Florida Geological Survey, Bulletin 25, figure 71, 1 sheet, 1:400,000 scale.

Devine, T.W., Roehl, E.A., Jr., and Busby, J.B., 2003, Virtual sensors—Cost effective monitoring, in Proceedings of the Air and Waste Management Association Annual Conference, June 2003: San Diego, CA.

Dutta, S., Wierenga, B., Dalebout, A., 1997, Case-based reasoning systems—From automation to decision-aiding and stimulation: IEEE Transactions on Knowledge and Data Engineering, v. 9, no. 6, p. 911–922.

Hinton, G.E., 1992, How neural networks learn from experience, Scientific American, v. 267, no. 3, p.145–151.

Jensen, B.A., 1994, Expert systems—Neural networks, in Lipták, B.G., ed., Process control, Instrument engineers' handbook (3d ed.): Boca Raton, FL, CRC Press, p. 48–54.

Meselhe, E.A., Griborio, A.G., and Shankar, Gautam, 2005, Hydrodynamic and water quality modeling for the A.R.M. Loxahatchee National Wildlife Refuge, Phase 1—Preparation of data: Lafayette, University of Louisiana at Lafayette, Report #LOXA05-014, accessed September 13, 2010, at *http://sofia.usgs.gov/lox_monitor_model/advisorypanel/ Data_Acquisition_and_Processing_Final_LOXA05-014.pdf.*

Richardson, J.R., Bryant, W.L., Kitchens, W.M., Mattson, J.E., and Pope, K.R., 1990, An evaluation of the refuge habitats and relationships to water quality, quantity, and hydroperiods—A synthesis report: Gainesville, FL, Florida Cooperative Fish and Wildlife Research Unit, University of Florida.

Risley, J.C., Roehl, E.A., Jr., and Conrads, P.A., 2003, Estimating water temperatures in small streams in western Oregon using neural network models: U.S. Geological Survey Water-Resources Investigations Report 02–4218, 59 p.

Roehl, E.A., Jr., Conrads, P.A., and Daamen, R.C., 2006b, Features of advanced decision support systems for environmental studies, management, and regulation, in Voinov, A., Jakeman, A.J., Rizzoli, A.E., eds., Proceedings of the iEMS Third Biennial Meeting—Summit on Environmental Modelling and Software, July 9–13, 2006, Burlington, VT: International Environmental Modelling and Software Society, CD–ROM, online at *http://www.iemss.org/ iemss2006/sessions/all.html*, accessed September 13, 2010.

Roehl, E.A., Conrads, P.A., and Roehl, T.A.S., 2000, Real-time control of the salt front in a complex, tidally affected river basin, in Smart engineering system design, Volume 10, Proceedings of the Artificial Neural Networks in Engineering Conference: New York, ASME Press, p. 947–954.

Roehl, Ed, Conrads, P.A., and Cook, J.B., 2003, Discussion of "Using complex permittivity and artificial neural networks for contaminant prediction" by John B. Lindsay, Julie Q. Shang, and R. Kerry Rowe: Journal of Environmental Engineering, v. 129, no. 11, p. 1069–1071.

Roehl, E.A., Risley, John, Stewart, Jana, and Mitro, Matthew, 2006a, Numerically optimized empirical modeling of highly dynamic, spatially expansive, and behaviorally heterogeneous hydrologic systems—Part 1, *in* Voinov, A., Jakeman, A.J., Rizzoli, A.E., eds., Proceedings of the iEMS Third Biennial Meeting—Summit on Environmental Modelling and Software, July 9–13, 2006, Burlington, VT: International Environmental Modelling and Software Society, CD–ROM, online at *http://www.iemss.org/ iemss2006/sessions/all.html*, accessed September 13, 2010.

Rosenblatt, Frank, 1958, The perceptron—A probabilistic model for information storage and organization in the brain: Psychological Review, v. 65, no. 6, p. 386–408.

Rumelhart, D.E., Hinton, G.E., and Williams, R.J., 1986, Learning internal representations by error propagation, *in* Rumelhart, D.E., McClelland, J.L., and the PDP Research Group, Parallel distributed processing—Explorations in the microstructure of cognition, Volume 1—Foundations: Cambridge, MA, MIT Press, p. 318–362.

U.S. Fish and Wildlife Service, 2000, Arthur R. Marshall Loxahatchee National Wildlife Refuge Comprehensive Conservation Plan, accessed September 13, 2010, at *http://loxahatchee.fws.gov.*

U.S. Fish and Wildlife Service, 2007a, A.R.M. Loxahatchee National Wildlife Refuge Enhanced Monitoring and Modeling Program—2nd annual report, February 2007: Boynton Beach, FL, U.S. Fish and Wildlife Service, LOXA06-008, 183 p.

U.S. Fish and Wildlife Service, 2007b, A.R.M. Loxahatchee National Wildlife Refuge Enhanced Water Quality Monitoring and Modeling Program—3rd annual report, October 2007: Boynton Beach, FL, U.S. Fish and Wildlife Service, LOXA07-005, 116 p.

U.S. Fish and Wildlife Service, 2009, A.R.M. Loxahatchee National Wildlife Refuge Enhanced Water Quality Program—4th annual report, July 2009: Boynton Beach, FL, U.S. Fish and Wildlife Service, LOXA09-007, 106 p.

Walker, W.W., Jr., 1995, Design basis for Everglades stormwater treatment areas: American Water Resources Association, Water Resources Bulletin, v. 31, no. 4, p. 671–685.

Weiss, S.M., and Indurkhya, Nitin, 1998, Predictive data mining—A practical guide: San Francisco, Morgan Kaufmann Publishers, Inc., 228 p.

Appendix 1. List of Variables Used in the Study

Appendix 1.   List of variables used in the study

Variable	Description
ET_A0	3-day moving window average of evapotranspiration (ET)
ET_A1	10-day moving window average of evapotranspiration (ET)
ET_A2	30-day moving window average of evapotranspiration (ET)
ET_A3	90-day moving window average of evapotranspiration (ET)
ET_A4	210-day moving window average of evapotranspiration (ET)
ET_A5	330-day moving window average of evapotranspiration (ET)
ET_D0	Difference between the 3-day and 10-day moving window average of evapotranspiration (ET)
ET_D1	Difference between the 10-day and 30-day moving window average of evapotranspiration (ET)
ET_D2	Difference between the 30-day and 90-day moving window average of evapotranspiration (ET)
ET_D3	Difference between the 90-day and 210-day moving window average of evapotranspiration (ET)
ET_D4	Difference between the 210-day and 330-day moving window average of evapotranspiration (ET)
F_GH_1-8C	Filled gage heights for the site 1-8C gaging station
GH_1-8C_D3	Difference between the 3-day and 9-day moving window average of site 1-8C gage heights
GH_1-8C_D30	Difference between the 30-day and 90-day moving window average of site 1-8C gage heights
GH_1-8C_D9	Difference between the 9-day and 30-day moving window average of site 1-8C gage heights
GH_1-8C_D90	Difference between the 90-day and 180-day moving window average of site 1-8C gage heights
GH_1-8T_D3	Difference between the 3-day and 9-day moving window average of site 1-8T gage heights
GH_1-8T_D30	Difference between the 30-day and 90-day moving window average of site 1-8T gage heights
GH_1-8T_D9	Difference between the 9-day and 30-day moving window average of site 1-8T gage heights
GH_1-8T_D90	Difference between the 90-day and 180-day moving window average of site 1-8T gage heights
GH-1-8C_A10	10-day moving window of site 1-8C gage height (GH)
GH-1-8C_A180	180-day moving window of site 1-8C gage height (GH)
GH-1-8C_A30	30-day moving window of site 1-8C gage height (GH)
GH-1-8C_A30	3-day moving window of site 1-8C gage height (GH)
GH-1-8C_A90	90-day moving window of site 1-8C gage height (GH)
GH-1-8T_A10	10-day moving window of site 1-8T gage height (GH)
GH-1-8T_A180	180-day moving window of site 1-8T gage height (GH)
GH-1-8T_A30	30-day moving window of site 1-8T gage height (GH)
GH-1-8T_A30	3-day moving window of site 1-8T gage height (GH)
GH-1-8T_A90	90-day moving window of site 1-8T gage height (GH)
GH-ERR	Difference between linear regression water-level model estimates and measured water levels
GH-LFITS	Gage height estimate from linear regression water-level models
N_GH_1-7_D3	Difference between the 3-day and 9-day moving window average of site 1-7 normalized gage heights
N_GH_1-7_D30	Difference between the 30-day and 90-day moving window average of site 1-7 normalized gage heights
N_GH_1-7_D9	Difference between the 9-day and 30-day moving window average of site 1-7 normalized gage heights
N_GH_1-7_D90	Difference between the 90-day and 180-day moving window average of site 1-7 normalized gage heights
N_GH_1-8C_D3	Difference between the 3-day and 9-day moving window average of site 1-8C normalized gage heights
N_GH_1-8C_D30	Difference between the 30-day and 90-day moving window average of site 1-8C normalized gage heights
N_GH_1-8C_D9	Difference between the 9-day and 30-day moving window average of site 1-8C normalized gage heights
N_GH_1-8C_D90	Difference between the 90-day and 180-day moving window average of site 1-8C normalized gage heights

Appendix 1.   List of variables used in the study.—Continued

Variable	Description
N_GH_1-9_D3	Difference between the 3-day and 9-day moving window average of site 1-9 normalized gage heights
N_GH_1-9_D30	Difference between the 30-day and 90-day moving window average of site 1-9 normalized gage heights
N_GH_1-9_D9	Difference between the 9-day and 30-day moving window average of site 1-9 normalized gage heights
N_GH_1-9_D90	Difference between the 90-day and 180-day moving window average of site 1-9 normalized gage heights
N_GH-1-7_A10	10-day moving window of site 1-7 normalized gage height (GH)
N_GH-1-7_A180	180-day moving window of site 1-7 normalized gage height (GH)
N_GH-1-7_A30	30-day moving window of site 1-7 normalized gage height (GH)
N_GH-1-7_A30	3-day moving window of site 1-7 normalized gage height (GH)
N_GH-1-7_A90	90-day moving window of site 1-7 normalized gage height (GH)
N_GH-1-8C_A10	10-day moving window of site 1-8C normalized gage height (GH)
N_GH-1-8C_A180	180-day moving window of site 1-8C normalized gage height (GH)
N_GH-1-8C_A30	30-day moving window of site 1-8C normalized gage height (GH)
N_GH-1-8C_A30	3-day moving window of site 1-8C normalized gage height (GH)
N_GH-1-8C_A90	90-day moving window of site 1-8C normalized gage height (GH)
N_GH-1-9_A10	10-day moving window of site 1-9 normalized gage height (GH)
N_GH-1-9_A180	180-day moving window of site 1-9 normalized gage height (GH)
N_GH-1-9_A30	30-day moving window of site 1-9 normalized gage height (GH)
N_GH-1-9_A30	3-day moving window of site 1-9 normalized gage height (GH)
N_GH-1-9_A90	90-day moving window of site 1-9 normalized gage height (GH)
Q1_A0	3-day moving window average of Q1 aggregated flows
Q1_A1	10-day moving window average of Q1 aggregated flows
Q1_A2	30-day moving window average of Q1 aggregated flows
Q1_A3	90-day moving window average of Q1 aggregated flows
Q1_A4	210-day moving window average of Q1 aggregated flows
Q1_A5	330-day moving window average of Q1 aggregated flows
Q1_D0	Difference between the 3-day and 10-day moving window average of Q1 aggregated flows
Q1_D1	Difference between the 10-day and 30-day moving window average of Q1 aggregated flows
Q1_D2	Difference between the 30-day and 90-day moving window average of Q1 aggregated flows
Q1_D3	Difference between the 90-day and 210-day moving window average of Q1 aggregated flows
Q1_D4	Difference between the 210-day and 330-day moving window average of Q1 aggregated flows
Q2_A0	3-day moving window average of Q2 aggregated flows
Q2_A1	10-day moving window average of Q2 aggregated flows
Q2_A2	30-day moving window average of Q2 aggregated flows
Q2_A3	90-day moving window average of Q2 aggregated flows
Q2_A4	210-day moving window average of Q2 aggregated flows
Q2_A5	330-day moving window average of Q2 aggregated flows
Q2_D0	Difference between the 3-day and 10-day moving window average of Q2 aggregated flows
Q2_D1	Difference between the 10-day and 30-day moving window average of Q2 aggregated flows
Q2_D2	Difference between the 30-day and 90-day moving window average of Q2 aggregated flows
Q2_D3	Difference between the 90-day and 210-day moving window average of Q2 aggregated flows

Appendix 1.   List of variables used in the study.—Continued

Variable	Description
Q2_D4	Difference between the 210-day and 330-day moving window average of Q2 aggregated flows
Q3_A0	3-day moving window average of Q3 aggregated flows
Q3_A1	10-day moving window average of Q3 aggregated flows
Q3_A2	30-day moving window average of Q3 aggregated flows
Q3_A3	90-day moving window average of Q3 aggregated flows
Q3_A4	210-day moving window average of Q3 aggregated flows
Q3_A5	330-day moving window average of Q3 aggregated flows
Q3_D0	Difference between the 3-day and 10-day moving window average of Q3 aggregated flows
Q3_D1	Difference between the 10-day and 30-day moving window average of Q3 aggregated flows
Q3_D2	Difference between the 30-day and 90-day moving window average of Q3 aggregated flows
Q3_D3	Difference between the 90-day and 210-day moving window average of Q3 aggregated flows
Q3_D4	Difference between the 210-day and 330-day moving window average of Q3 aggregated flows
Q4_A0	3-day moving window average of Q4 aggregated flows
Q4_A1	10-day moving window average of Q4 aggregated flows
Q4_A2	30-day moving window average of Q4 aggregated flows
Q4_A3	90-day moving window average of Q4 aggregated flows
Q4_A4	210-day moving window average of Q4 aggregated flows
Q4_A5	330-day moving window average of Q4 aggregated flows
Q4_D0	Difference between the 3-day and 10-day moving window average of Q4 aggregated flows
Q4_D1	Difference between the 10-day and 30-day moving window average of Q4 aggregated flows
Q4_D2	Difference between the 30-day and 90-day moving window average of Q4 aggregated flows
Q4_D3	Difference between the 90-day and 210-day moving window average of Q4 aggregated flows
Q4_D4	Difference between the 210-day and 330-day moving window average of Q4 aggregated flows
Q5_A0	3-day moving window average of Q5 aggregated flows
Q5_A1	10-day moving window average of Q5 aggregated flows
Q5_A2	30-day moving window average of Q5 aggregated flows
Q5_A3	90-day moving window average of Q5 aggregated flows
Q5_A4	210-day moving window average of Q5 aggregated flows
Q5_A5	330-day moving window average of Q5 aggregated flows
Q5_D0	Difference between the 3-day and 10-day moving window average of Q5 aggregated flows
Q5_D1	Difference between the 10-day and 30-day moving window average of Q5 aggregated flows
Q5_D2	Difference between the 30-day and 90-day moving window average of Q5 aggregated flows
Q5_D3	Difference between the 90-day and 210-day moving window average of Q5 aggregated flows
Q5_D4	Difference between the 210-day and 330-day moving window average of Q5 aggregated flows
Q6_A0	3-day moving window average of Q6 aggregated flows
Q6_A1	10-day moving window average of Q6 aggregated flows
Q6_A2	30-day moving window average of Q6 aggregated flows
Q6_A3	90-day moving window average of Q6 aggregated flows
Q6_A4	210-day moving window average of Q6 aggregated flows
Q6_A5	330-day moving window average of Q6 aggregated flows

Appendix 1. List of variables used in the study.—Continued

Variable	Description
Q6_D0	Difference between the 3-day and 10-day moving window average of Q6 aggregated flows
Q6_D1	Difference between the 10-day and 30-day moving window average of Q6 aggregated flows
Q6_D2	Difference between the 30-day and 90-day moving window average of Q6 aggregated flows
Q6_D3	Difference between the 90-day and 210-day moving window average of Q6 aggregated flows
Q6_D4	Difference between the 210-day and 330-day moving window average of Q6 aggregated flows
R_SC	Residual time series computed from static spatially interpolating specific conductance model
R_TP	Residual time series computed from static spatially interpolating total phosphorus model
RAIN_A0	3-day moving window average of rainfall
RAIN_A1	10-day moving window average of rainfall
RAIN_A2	30-day moving window average of rainfall
RAIN_A3	90-day moving window average of rainfall
RAIN_A4	210-day moving window average of rainfall
RAIN_A5	330-day moving window average of rainfall
RAIN_D0	Difference between the 3-day and 10-day moving window average of rainfall
RAIN_D1	Difference between the 10-day and 30-day moving window average of rainfall
RAIN_D2	Difference between the 30-day and 90-day moving window average of rainfall
RAIN_D3	Difference between the 90-day and 210-day moving window average of rainfall
RAIN_D4	Difference between the 210-day and 330-day moving window average of rainfall
RAIN-ET-COMB_A180	180-day moving window average of the combined rainfall and evapotranspiration variable
RAIN-ET-COMB_A3	3-day moving window average of the combined rainfall and evapotranspiration variable
RAIN-ET-COMB_A30	30-day moving window average of the combined rainfall and evapotranspiration variable
RAIN-ET-COMB_A9	9-day moving window average of the combined rainfall and evapotranspiration variable
RAIN-ET-COMB_A90	90-day moving window average of the combined rainfall and evapotranspiration variable
RAIN-ET-COMB_D3	Difference between the 3-day and 9-day moving window average of combined rainfall and evapotranspiration variable
RAIN-ET-COMB_D30	Difference between the 30-day and 90-day moving window average of combined rainfall and evapotranspiration variable
RAIN-ET-COMB_D9	Difference between the 9-day and 30-day moving window average of combined rainfall and evapotranspiration variable
RAIN-ET-COMB_D90	Difference between the 90-day and 180-day moving window average of combined rainfall and evapotranspiration variable
S39-SC_I90_A10	10-day moving window average of the 90-day interpolated specific conductance concentration at the S-39 control structure
S39-SC_I90_A180	180-day moving window average of the 90-day interpolated specific conductance concentration at the S-39 control structure
S39-SC_I90_A30	30-day moving window average of the 90-day interpolated specific conductance concentration at the S-39 control structure
S39-SC_I90_A30	3-day moving window average of the 90-day interpolated specific conductance concentration at the S-39 control structure
S39-SC_I90_A90	90-day moving window average of the 90-day interpolated specific conductance concentration at the S-39 control structure
S39-SC_I90_D10	Difference between the 10-day and 30-day moving window average of interpolated specific conductance concentration at the S-39 control structure

Appendix 1.   List of variables used in the study.—Continued

Variable	Description
S39-SC_I90_D3	Difference between the 3-day and 10-day moving window average of interpolated specific conductance concentration at the S-39 control structure
S39-SC_I90_D30	Difference between the 30-day and 90-day moving window average of interpolated specific conductance concentration at the S-39 control structure
S39-SC_I90_D90	Difference between the 90-day and 180-day moving window average of interpolated specific conductance concentration at the S-39 control structure
S6-TP_I90_A10	10-day moving window average of the 90-day interpolated total phosphorus concentration at the S-6 control structure
S6-TP_I90_A180	180-day moving window average of the 90-day interpolated total phosphorus concentration at the S-6 control structure
S6-TP_I90_A30	30-day moving window average of the 90-day interpolated total phosphorus concentration at the S-6 control structure
S6-TP_I90_A30	3-day moving window average of the 90-day interpolated total phosphorus concentration at the S-6 control structure
S6-TP_I90_A90	90-day moving window average of the 90-day interpolated total phosphorus concentration at the S-6 control structure
S6-TP_I90_D10	Difference between the 10-day and 30-day moving window average of interpolated total phosphorus concentration at the S-6 control structure
S6-TP_I90_D3	Difference between the 3-day and 10-day moving window average of interpolated total phosphorus concentration at the S-6 control structure
S6-TP_I90_D30	Difference between the 30-day and 90-day moving window average of interpolated total phosphorus concentration at the S-6 control structure
S6-TP_I90_D90	Difference between the 90-day and 180-day moving window average of interpolated total phosphorus concentration at the S-6 control structure
SC	Total phosphorus at the XYZ sampling sites—stacked variable
TOTQ_A0	3-day moving window average of total flow (TOTQ)
TOTQ_A1	10-day moving window average of total flow (TOTQ)
TOTQ_A2	30-day moving window average of total flow (TOTQ)
TOTQ_A3	90-day moving window average of total flow (TOTQ)
TOTQ_A4	210-day moving window average of total flow (TOTQ)
TOTQ_A5	330-day moving window average of total flow (TOTQ)
TOTQ_D0	Difference between the 3-day and 10-day moving window average of total flow (TOTQ)
TOTQ_D1	Difference between the 10-day and 30-day moving window average of total flow (TOTQ)
TOTQ_D2	Difference between the 30-day and 90-day moving window average of total flow (TOTQ)
TOTQ_D3	Difference between the 90-day and 210-day moving window average of total flow (TOTQ)
TOTQ_D4	Difference between the 210-day and 330-day moving window average of total flow (TOTQ)
TP	Specific conductance at the LOX and XYZ sampling sites—stacked variable
X	X location of gaging station or water quality sampling site
Y	Y location of gaging station or water quality sampling site

Appendix 2. User's Manual for the LOXahatchee Artificial Neural Network Decision Support System (LOXANN DSS)

Figures

Tables

1. Introduction

This document describes how to install and operate an empirical model (LOXANN DSS) of the Arthur R. Marshall Loxahatchee National Wildlife Refuge (Refuge). LOXANN is a decision support system (DSS) built around a suite of empirical hydrologic and water-quality models.

2. LOXMODEL Installation, Removal, and Technical Assistance

NOTE: LOXANN will not run on 64-bit Windows XP® and Vista® operating systems because of incompatibility of the NNCALC32.xll Add-in with these operating systems. NNCALC32.xll is used to execute the Artificial Neural Network (ANN) models.

2.1. Installation

1. Create a folder called LOXMODEL at the top level of your C: drive.

2. Extract all files from LOXMODEL-yyyymmdd.zip[1] from the CD–ROM provided by the USGS into the LOXMODEL folder. The zip file contains the following application files:

    *   LOXMODEL-yyyymmdd.xls—A Microsoft (MS) Excel® spreadsheet application.

    *   Files with an "enn" extension are the ANN files—there are five ANN files:

        1. p_gh_errs-use.enn

        2. p_sc-use.enn

        3. p_r_sc-use.enn

        4. p_tp-use.enn

        5. p_r_tp-use.enn

    *   NNCALC32.xll—An MS Excel Add-in used to execute the ANN model (*.enn) files.

    *   LOXMODELUserGuide-yyyymmdd.doc—The MS Word® file that you are reading right now.

    *   LOXMODEL-Install-yyyymmdd.doc—An MS Word file with these installation instructions.

3. Open your copy of MS Excel® for MS Office 2000® (or newer). Ensure that the standard Excel Add-ins listed below are installed and checked "available."

    Analysis Toolpak

    Analysis Toolpak—VBA

    Add-ins are accessed from Excel's Tools menu. If any are missing, it may be necessary to install them from your MS Office CD–ROM.

4. Set the macro security level of Excel to either medium or low using Tools > Macro > Security. LOXANN uses VBA macros for a variety of purposes and must be able to execute them to operate correctly.

5. Install the NNCALC32 Add-in that resides in the NNCALC folder described in Step 1. This may be accomplished by clicking on Tools > Add-ins > Browse, browse to the LOXMODEL folder you created, click on the NNCALC32 icon, then click OK.

6. Open the LOXMODEL-yyyymmdd.xls Excel spreadsheet application. When Excel asks if you want to run macros click "Enable Macros," otherwise LOXMODEL will not operate correctly.

---

[1] yyyymmdd is the version date of the LOXMODEL image to be installed.

Select the "Controls" worksheet (fig. 2–1). "Controls" is the worksheet that lets the user set up and run simulations. At the top-left corner of "Controls" is a text box labeled "Path Where ANN Model Files Are Located." The model files are the *.enn files of the ANNs. Type in the fully qualified path name of the folder setup in (1) above and save the Excel application using File > Save for the setup changes to be permanent.

Just below the text box is a field labeled "ANNs Connected." This field will have a value = "TRUE" if the application is properly configured and ready to use. If the field is blank, try exiting Excel and reopening Excel and the LOXMODEL application.

A blank field indicates that one or more ANNs cannot execute because either the NNCALC32 Add-in is not installed per (5) or NNCALC32 cannot find *.enn files because the folder path name in the "Where model files are located" text box is incorrect.

If you cannot get LOXMODEL to operate, re-check the configuration items in (3)–(6) above.

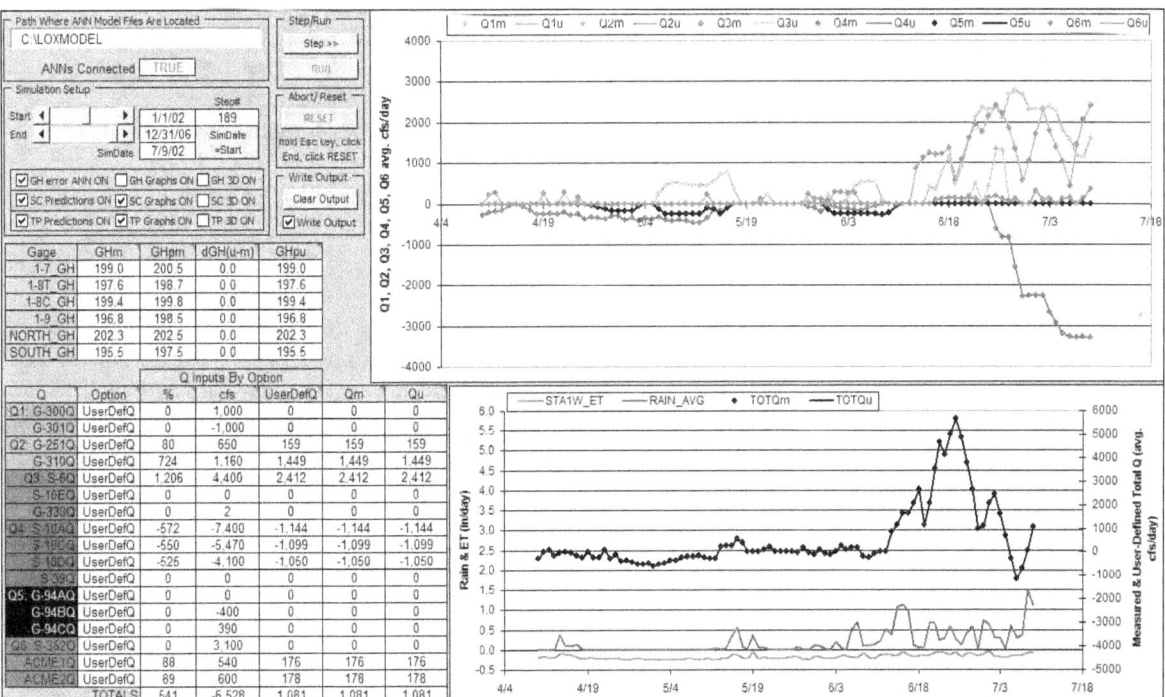

Figure 2–1.   Screenshot of "Controls" worksheet.

2.2. Removal

Simply delete the folder created to hold the LOXANN DSS files and its contents. Consider removing the Add-ins and reverting to the default MS Excel security settings.

2.3. Technical Assistance

Please contact Paul Conrads of the USGS at (803) 750-6140, pconrads@usgs.gov, if you have questions or problems with LOXANN DSS.

3. LOXANN DSS Features and Operation

LOXMODEL is opened like any standard Excel workbook. Simply open the LOXMODEL-yyyymmdd.xls file and you are ready to go. LOXANN DSS and its graphical user interface (GUI) are made up of a number of worksheets that are detailed below.

3.1. Parameter Descriptions, Nomenclature, and "ReleaseNotes" Worksheet

LOXANN refers to many input and output parameters usually in the form of column headers (fig. 2–2). Moving the mouse over a header marked with a red caret in the right hand corner of the header will provide a description of the header parameter.

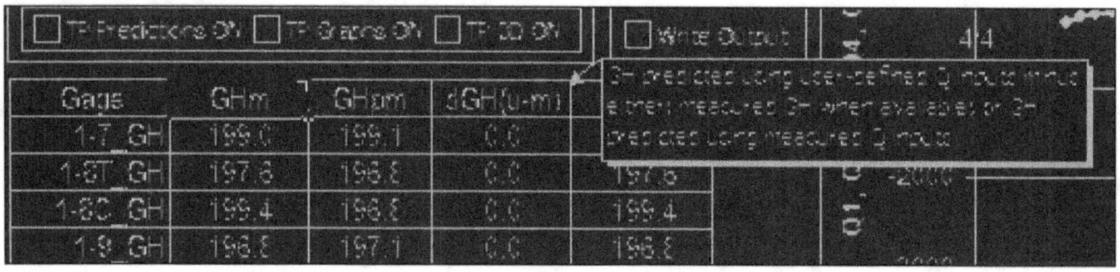

Figure 2–2.   On-line description of parameter dGH(u-m) on the "Run" worksheet.

Descriptions of parameters also are provided in the "ReleaseNotes" worksheet. This worksheet describes changes made in different releases of LOXANN's development history and any new features. Some of the prefixes, suffixes, and other modifiers that are used in parameter names include

- "d": used as a prefix to indicate that the parameter is a difference between two other parameter values

- "p": used to indicate that the parameter is a model prediction

- "m": used to indicate that the parameter's value is either

  ○ an actual measurement

  ○ a model prediction made using an actual measurement as an input value

- "u": used to indicate that a parameter's value is set by the user.

Modifiers can be used in combination, for example, dGH(u-m) as shown in figure 2–2.

3.2. "Info" Worksheet

The "Info" worksheet is automatically displayed when LOXANN is first loaded (fig. 2–3). It contains the program's version date and the contact information of its developers.

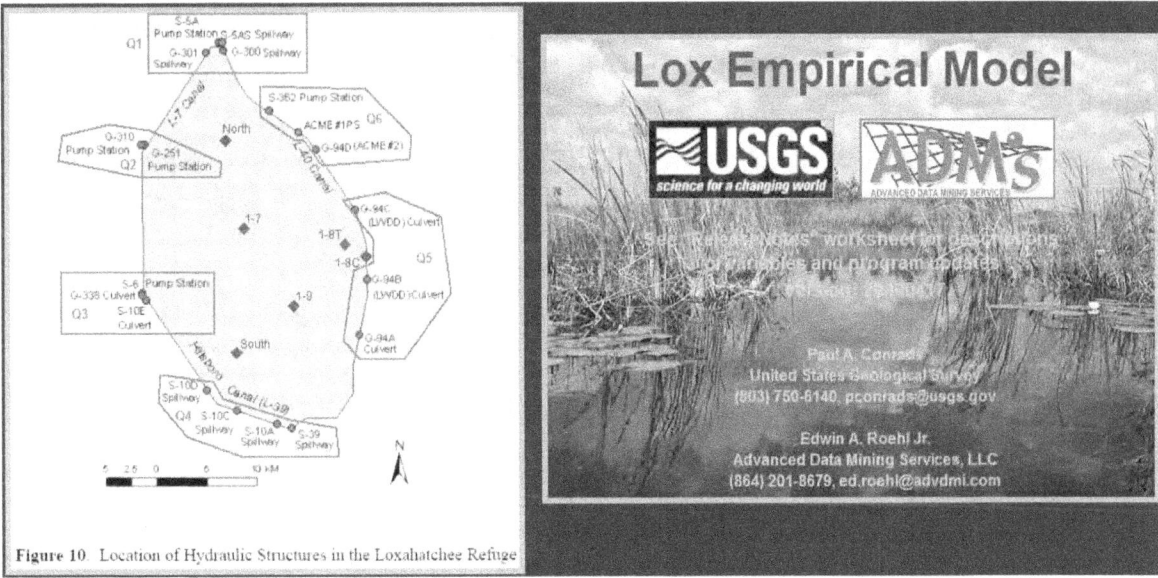

Figure 2–3. "Info" worksheet.

3.3. "Controls" Worksheet

The "Controls" worksheet (fig. 2–4) is the GUI component that lets the user setup and run simulations.

A text box labeled "Path Where ANN Model Files Are Located" (fig. 2–4) is located on the "Controls" worksheet. It is used to configure LOXANN when it is first installed on a user's computer and is described further in section 4. The "Start" and "End" dates for simulations can be set using the scroll bars at center left. The end date must be more recent than the start date. The "SimDate" field indicates the time stamp for which LOXANN's models are currently generating output values. The "Step#" is an integer counter that indicates how many time steps (days) have been executed since the start of a simulation. The "SimDate=Start" button sets the current time stamp to the Simulation "Start" date. The "Step>>" button increases the current time stamp by one time step.

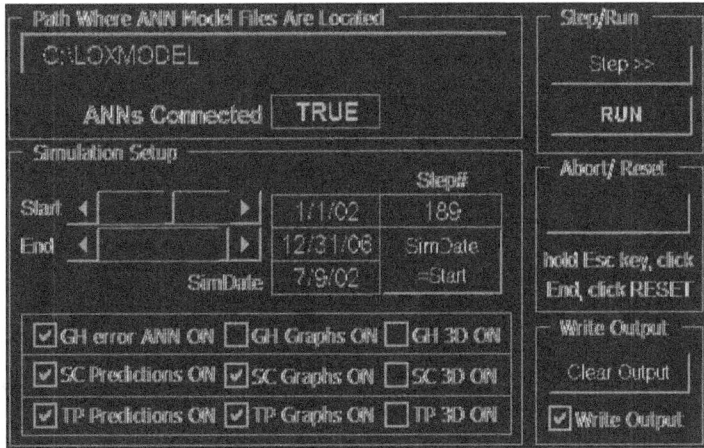

Figure 2–4. Simulation controls on "Controls" worksheet.

The "RUN" button will start and run a simulation between the dates indicated by the Simulation "Start" and "End" dates. A simulation may be stopped at any time during a run by holding down the "Esc" key, after which a pop-up window will appear like that shown in figure 2–5. Click on the "End" button to stop the simulation, then click the "Reset" button shown at center right in figure 2–4. The user will not need to use other options (Continue, Debug, or Help) on the pop-up window. The "Reset" button activates Excel's automatic calculation feature (autocalc). Because the model programmatically manipulates autocalc for performance reasons, interrupting a simulation can sometimes leave the model in a state where autocalc is not activated. This is remedied by clicking the "Reset" button.

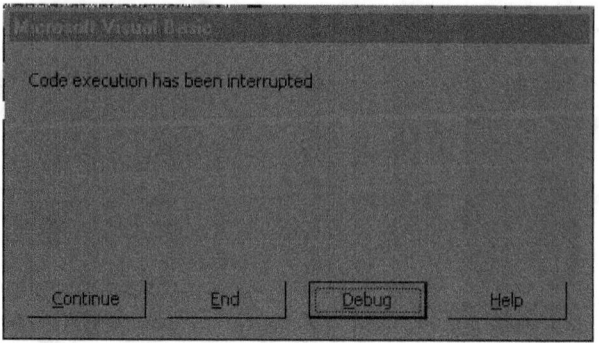

Figure 2–5.   Pop-up window that appears when a simulation is interrupted by using the "Esc" key.

LOXANN provides detailed numerical and streaming graphical information that can be observed during simulations or when incrementally stepping through time. This allows the user to examine specific periods and behaviors of interest in detail. Because of the added computational load, simulations are slowed as more models are activated, and streaming graphics and simulation output are generated. To speed calculations and the generation of output, a number of check boxes (lower left in figure 2–4) allow the user to activate/deactivate models, LOXANN's graphics features, and write model input and output data.

The gage height (GH) linear models are always active because their output is required by the specific conductance (SC) and total phosphorus (TP) models. The spatially interpolating artificial neural network model (SIANN) that partially corrects for the prediction error ε_{GH} of the linear GH models is toggled ON/OFF using the "GH error ANN ON" box. The SC and TP models are toggled using the "…Predictions ON" boxes. Trend graphs on the "Input Graphs" and "GH Graphs" are toggled using the "GH Graphs ON" box. Trend graphs on the "SC Graphs" and "TP Graphs" are toggled using the "SC Graphs ON" and "TP Graphs ON" boxes, respectively. Three-dimensional (3D) color gradient displays of GHs and SC and TP concentrations on the "3DVis" worksheet are toggled using the "… 3D ON" boxes.

A minimum of 330 days (time steps) of control structure flow values is required for the GH model to execute because the model uses moving window averages up to that size to simulate GH dynamics. The measured data for most structures is complete; however, the data for the G-94A, G-94B, and G-94C (summed into Q5) are missing prior to April 15, 2000. Thus, GH model runs that use the "use%" Input Option will not execute until 330 time steps after this date, which is March 10, 2001. The GH model will execute for earlier dates when using user options "cfs" and "UserDefQ" for G-94A, G-94B, and G-94C on the "Q Setpoints" worksheet because the user inputs for these sites are then purely synthetic (see Section 3.4).

A minimum of 180 time steps of GH predictions is required for the SC and TP models to execute because the models use moving window averages up to that size to simulate SC and TP dynamics. Therefore, the total requirement in terms of run time before SC and TP predictions are made is 330 time steps for the GH model plus 180 time steps for the SC and TP models. Use the displayed "Step#" value (fig. 2–4) on the "Controls" and other worksheets to assist in setting up and monitoring simulations.

LOXANN also will write input and output data to the "Output" worksheet. The "Write Output" check box at the lower right in figure 2–4 toggles this feature. The "Clear Output" button erases all data in the "Output" worksheet to allow data from a new simulation to be recorded.

Figure 2–6 shows the GH information fields on the "Controls" worksheet. By site location, the GHm column shows the measured GHs for the current time step. The GHpm column shows the predicted GH values made by the GH model while using measured control structure flows for input data. Whether or not the GH error correction ANN model ("GH error ANN ON," fig. 2–4) is activated will affect these values. The dGH(u-m) column shows the predicted GH using user-defined Q inputs minus either the measured GH, when available, or the GH predicted using measured Q inputs when the measured GH is unavailable. The GHpu column shows dGH(u-m) plus either the measured GH, when available, or the GH predicted using measured Q inputs.

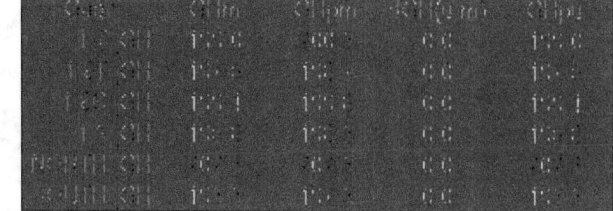

Figure 2–6.   GH fields on "Controls" worksheet.

Figure 2–7 shows the control structure flow information fields on the "Controls" worksheet. By structure, the Option column shows the input flow option selected by the user on the "Q Setpoints" worksheet. The %, cfs, and UserDefQ columns show what the user-set flow input values would be for the current time step if Option was set at %, cfs, or UserDefQ, respectively. The user-set input flow values also are set on "Q Setpoints." The Qm column shows the current measured flows. The Qu column shows which of the input flow options (%, cfs, or UserDefQ) is being input per the Option setting.

Figure 2–7. Q fields on "Controls" worksheet.

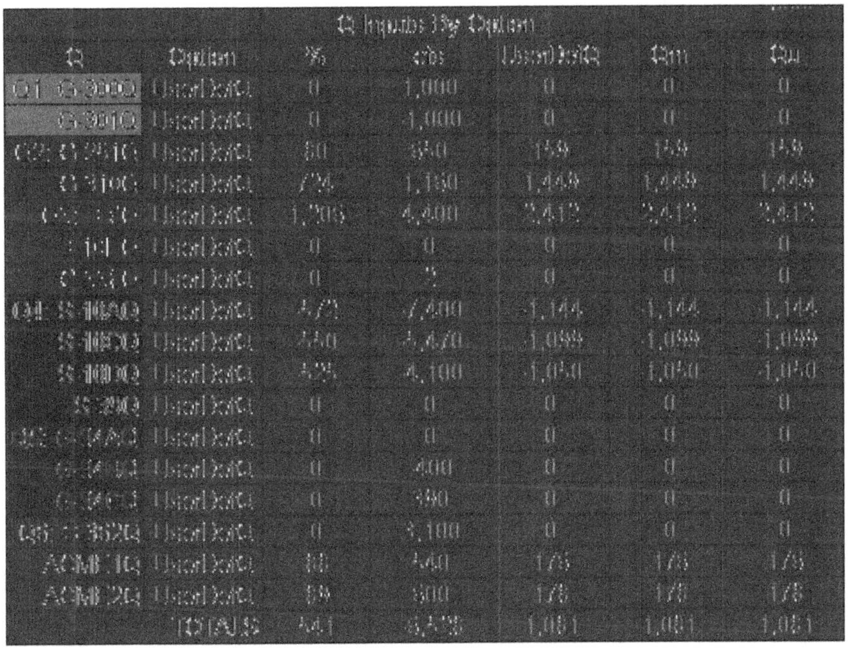

3.4. "Q Setpoints" Worksheet

Figure 2–8 shows the upper portion of the "Q Setpoints" worksheet, which is the component of LOXANN's GUI that allows the user to set flow setpoints for each control structure. Actual setpoint values used for each structure are determined by the associated scroll bars. By structure, the scroll bars in the "Input Option" column are used to select the type of user-set input to use. The type selected is shown in a field immediately above each scroll bar. The "%" option multiplies the measured flow by a percentage set using the % scroll bar shown at the right in figure 2–8. The "cfs" option sets the flow to a constant value in units of cubic feet per second using the cfs scroll bar immediately below the % scroll bar. The "UserDefQ" option causes LOXANN to read values from a flow time series copied by the user into the "UserDefQs" worksheet. To minimize the extrapolation of the models to conditions much different than those used to train the models, the "Q Setpoints" worksheet also lists the historical maximum and minimum values for each structure during the study period, and upper and lower limits allowed for the user setting.

Figure 2–8. Upper portion of "Q Setpoints" worksheet.

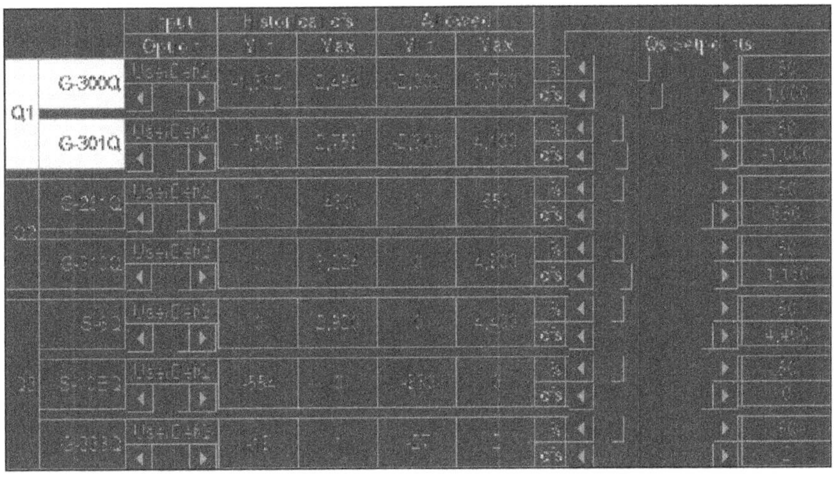

3.5. "Database" and "Output" Worksheets

The "Database" worksheet contains the measured data used by LOXANN to run simulations (fig. 2–9). These data are described in table 2–1 and are derived from the raw field measurements. The data are augmented by calculated parameters, the values of which are calculated "on-the-fly" by LOXANN's computer code. The user should not alter data in the "Database" worksheet.

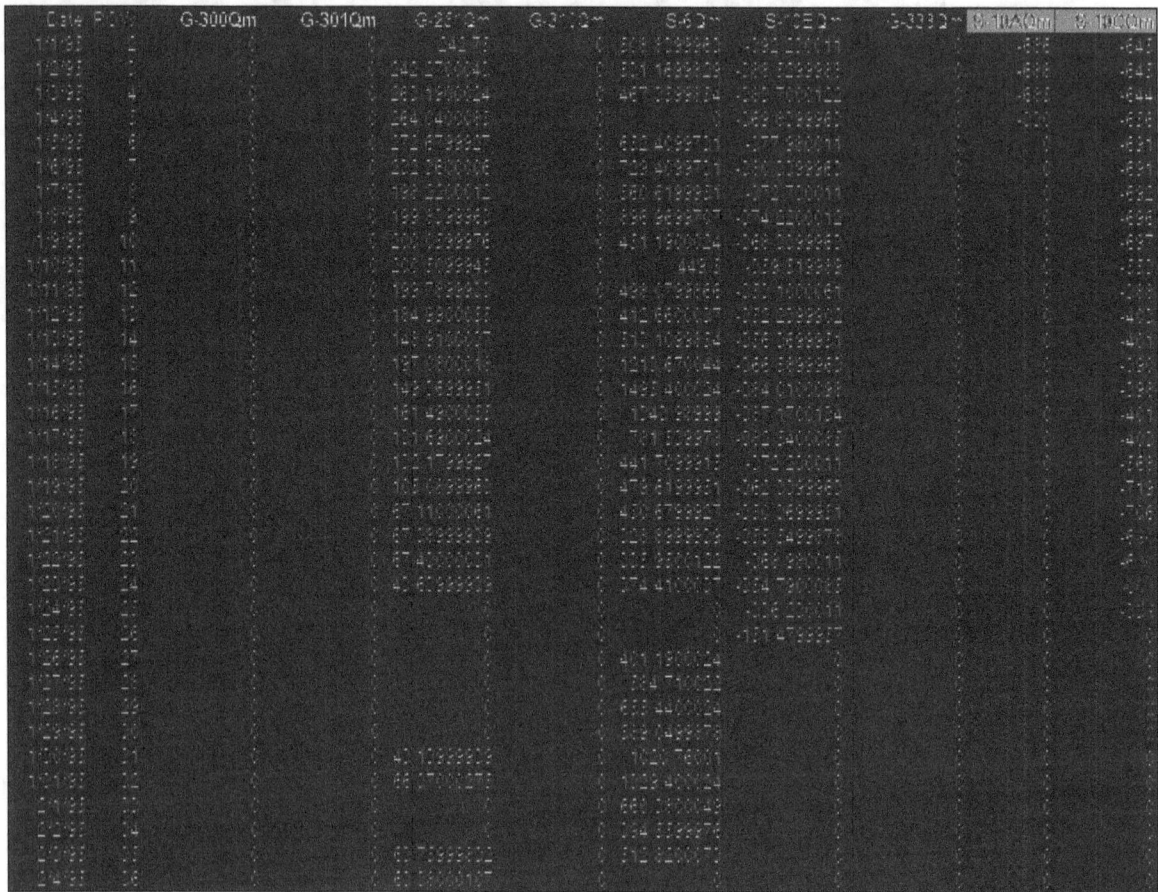

Figure 2–9. Example of measured data from the "Database" worksheet.

Table 2–1. Descriptions of "Database" worksheet parameters.

LOXANN writes a record of key parameters for a particular simulation run to the "Output" worksheet (fig. 2–10). The "Write Output" check box on the "Controls" worksheet must be checked for output to be written. The parameters written to the "Output" worksheet are described in table 2–2. The user can copy output values into another Excel workbook for further analysis. The "Clear Output" button located on the "Controls" worksheet erases all data in the "Output" worksheet to allow data from a new simulation to be recorded.

Figure 2–10.   Example output from the "Output" worksheet showing user-set control structure flows.

Table 2–2. Descriptions of "OUTPUT" worksheet parameters.

NAME	DESCRIPTION	NAME	DESCRIPTION
G-300Qu-opt	user-set input flow option for indicated control structure	XC-SCm	measured SC at indicated site
G-301Qu-opt	user-set input flow option for indicated control structure	XC-SCpm	predicted SC at indicated site using input measured flow
G-251Qu-opt	user-set input flow option for indicated control structure	XC-SCpu	predicted SC at indicated site using input user-set flow
G-310Qu-opt	user-set input flow option for indicated control structure	X1-SCm	measured SC at indicated site
S-6Qu-opt	user-set input flow option for indicated control structure	X1-SCpm	predicted SC at indicated site using input measured flow
S-10EQu-opt	user-set input flow option for indicated control structure	X1-SCpu	predicted SC at indicated site using input user-set flow
G-338Qu-opt	user-set input flow option for indicated control structure	X2-SCm	measured SC at indicated site
S-10AQu-opt	user-set input flow option for indicated control structure	X2-SCpm	predicted SC at indicated site using input measured flow
S-10CQu-opt	user-set input flow option for indicated control structure	X2-SCpu	predicted SC at indicated site using input user-set flow
S-10DQu-opt	user-set input flow option for indicated control structure	X3-SCm	measured SC at indicated site
S-39Qu-opt	user-set input flow option for indicated control structure	X3-SCpm	predicted SC at indicated site using input measured flow
G-94AQu-opt	user-set input flow option for indicated control structure	X3-SCpu	predicted SC at indicated site using input user-set flow
G-94BQu-opt	user-set input flow option for indicated control structure	X4-SCm	measured SC at indicated site
G-94CQu-opt	user-set input flow option for indicated control structure	X4-SCpm	predicted SC at indicated site using input measured flow
S-362Qu-opt	user-set input flow option for indicated control structure	X4-SCpu	predicted SC at indicated site using input user-set flow
ACME1Qu-opt	user-set input flow option for indicated control structure	Y4-SCm	measured SC at indicated site
ACME2Qu-opt	user-set input flow option for indicated control structure	Y4-SCpm	predicted SC at indicated site using input measured flow
G-300Qu	user-set input flow value for indicated control structure	Y4-SCpu	predicted SC at indicated site using input user-set flow
G-301Qu	user-set input flow value for indicated control structure	ZC-SCm	measured SC at indicated site
G-251Qu	user-set input flow value for indicated control structure	ZC-SCpm	predicted SC at indicated site using input measured flow
G-310Qu	user-set input flow value for indicated control structure	ZC-SCpu	predicted SC at indicated site using input user-set flow
S-6Qu	user-set input flow value for indicated control structure	Z1-SCm	measured SC at indicated site
S-10EQu	user-set input flow value for indicated control structure	Z1-SCpm	predicted SC at indicated site using input measured flow
G-338Qu	user-set input flow value for indicated control structure	Z1-SCpu	predicted SC at indicated site using input user-set flow
S-10AQu	user-set input flow value for indicated control structure	Z2-SCm	measured SC at indicated site
S-10CQu	user-set input flow value for indicated control structure	Z2-SCpm	predicted SC at indicated site using input measured flow
S-10DQu	user-set input flow value for indicated control structure	Z2-SCpu	predicted SC at indicated site using input user-set flow
S-39Qu	user-set input flow value for indicated control structure	Z3-SCm	measured SC at indicated site
G-94AQu	user-set input flow value for indicated control structure	Z3-SCpm	predicted SC at indicated site using input measured flow
G-94BQu	user-set input flow value for indicated control structure	Z3-SCpu	predicted SC at indicated site using input user-set flow
G-94CQu	user-set input flow value for indicated control structure	Z4-SCm	measured SC at indicated site
S-362Qu	user-set input flow value for indicated control structure	Z4-SCpm	predicted SC at indicated site using input measured flow
ACME1Qu	user-set input flow value for indicated control structure	Z4-SCpu	predicted SC at indicated site using input user-set flow
ACME2Qu	user-set input flow value for indicated control structure	LOX3-SCm	measured SC at indicated site
1-7_GHpm	GH model prediction at indicated site using input measured flow	LOX3-SCpm	predicted SC at indicated site using input measured flow
1-8T_GHpm	GH model prediction at indicated site using input measured flow	LOX3-SCpu	predicted SC at indicated site using input user-set flow
F_1-8C_GHpm	GH model prediction at indicated site using input measured flow	LOX4-SCm	measured SC at indicated site
1-9_GHpm	GH model prediction at indicated site using input measured flow	LOX4-SCpm	predicted SC at indicated site using input measured flow
NORTH_GHpm	GH model prediction at indicated site using input measured flow	LOX4-SCpu	predicted SC at indicated site using input user-set flow
SOUTH_GHpm	GH model prediction at indicated site using input measured flow	LOX5-SCm	measured SC at indicated site
1-7_GHpu	GH model prediction at indicated site using input user-set flow	LOX5-SCpm	predicted SC at indicated site using input measured flow
1-8T_GHpu	GH model prediction at indicated site using input user-set flow	LOX5-SCpu	predicted SC at indicated site using input user-set flow
F_1-8C_GHpu	GH model prediction at indicated site using input user-set flow	LOX6-SCm	measured SC at indicated site
1-9_GHpu	GH model prediction at indicated site using input user-set flow	LOX6-SCpm	predicted SC at indicated site using input measured flow
NORTH_GHpu	GH model prediction at indicated site using input user-set flow	LOX6-SCpu	predicted SC at indicated site using input user-set flow
SOUTH_GHpu	GH model prediction at indicated site using input user-set flow		

NAME	DESCRIPTION	NAME	DESCRIPTION
LOX7-SCm	measured SC at indicated site	LOX5-TPm	measured TP at indicated site
LOX7-SCpm	predicted SC at indicated site using input measured flow	LOX5-TPpm	predicted TP at indicated site using input measured flow
LOX7-SCpu	predicted SC at indicated site using input user-set flow	LOX5-TPpu	predicted TP at indicated site using input user-set flow
LOX8-SCm	measured SC at indicated site	LOX6-TPm	measured TP at indicated site
LOX8-SCpm	predicted SC at indicated site using input measured flow	LOX6-TPpm	predicted TP at indicated site using input measured flow
LOX8-SCpu	predicted SC at indicated site using input user-set flow	LOX6-TPpu	predicted TP at indicated site using input user-set flow
LOX9-SCm	measured SC at indicated site	LOX7-TPm	measured TP at indicated site
LOX9-SCpm	predicted SC at indicated site using input measured flow	LOX7-TPpm	predicted TP at indicated site using input measured flow
LOX9-SCpu	predicted SC at indicated site using input user-set flow	LOX7-TPpu	predicted TP at indicated site using input user-set flow
LOX10-SCm	measured SC at indicated site	LOX8-TPm	measured TP at indicated site
LOX10-SCpm	predicted SC at indicated site using input measured flow	LOX8-TPpm	predicted TP at indicated site using input measured flow
LOX10-SCpu	predicted SC at indicated site using input user-set flow	LOX8-TPpu	predicted TP at indicated site using input user-set flow
LOX11-SCm	measured SC at indicated site	LOX9-TPm	measured TP at indicated site
LOX11-SCpm	predicted SC at indicated site using input measured flow	LOX9-TPpm	predicted TP at indicated site using input measured flow
LOX11-SCpu	predicted SC at indicated site using input user-set flow	LOX9-TPpu	predicted TP at indicated site using input user-set flow
LOX12-SCm	measured SC at indicated site	LOX10-TPm	measured TP at indicated site
LOX12-SCpm	predicted SC at indicated site using input measured flow	LOX10-TPpm	predicted TP at indicated site using input measured flow
LOX12-SCpu	predicted SC at indicated site using input user-set flow	LOX10-TPpu	predicted TP at indicated site using input user-set flow
LOX13-SCm	measured SC at indicated site	LOX11-TPm	measured TP at indicated site
LOX13-SCpm	predicted SC at indicated site using input measured flow	LOX11-TPpm	predicted TP at indicated site using input measured flow
LOX13-SCpu	predicted SC at indicated site using input user-set flow	LOX11-TPpu	predicted TP at indicated site using input user-set flow
LOX14-SCm	measured SC at indicated site	LOX12-TPm	measured TP at indicated site
LOX14-SCpm	predicted SC at indicated site using input measured flow	LOX12-TPpm	predicted TP at indicated site using input measured flow
LOX14-SCpu	predicted SC at indicated site using input user-set flow	LOX12-TPpu	predicted TP at indicated site using input user-set flow
LOX15-SCm	measured SC at indicated site	LOX13-TPm	measured TP at indicated site
LOX15-SCpm	predicted SC at indicated site using input measured flow	LOX13-TPpm	predicted TP at indicated site using input measured flow
LOX15-SCpu	predicted SC at indicated site using input user-set flow	LOX13-TPpu	predicted TP at indicated site using input user-set flow
LOX16-SCm	measured SC at indicated site	LOX14-TPm	measured TP at indicated site
LOX16-SCpm	predicted SC at indicated site using input measured flow	LOX14-TPpm	predicted TP at indicated site using input measured flow
LOX16-SCpu	predicted SC at indicated site using input user-set flow	LOX14-TPpu	predicted TP at indicated site using input user-set flow
LOX3-TPm	measured TP at indicated site	LOX15-TPm	measured TP at indicated site
LOX3-TPpm	predicted TP at indicated site using input measured flow	LOX15-TPpm	predicted TP at indicated site using input measured flow
LOX3-TPpu	predicted TP at indicated site using input user-set flow	LOX15-TPpu	predicted TP at indicated site using input user-set flow
LOX4-TPm	measured TP at indicated site	LOX16-TPm	measured TP at indicated site
LOX4-TPpm	predicted TP at indicated site using input measured flow	LOX16-TPpm	predicted TP at indicated site using input measured flow
LOX4-TPpu	predicted TP at indicated site using input user-set flow	LOX16-TPpu	predicted TP at indicated site using input user-set flow

3.6. "UserDefQs" Worksheet

The "UserDefQs" worksheet allows the user to create customized flow time series for each control structure and have them run as the user-set inputs during simulations (fig. 2–11). The time series are simply pasted into the "UserDefQs" worksheet and individually activated for the control structure flows when their Input Option is set to "UserDefQ." The time series must be time-synchronized with the dates shown in the "DATE" column at the left. Options for each structure are set to "UserDefQ" on the "Q Setpoints" worksheet.

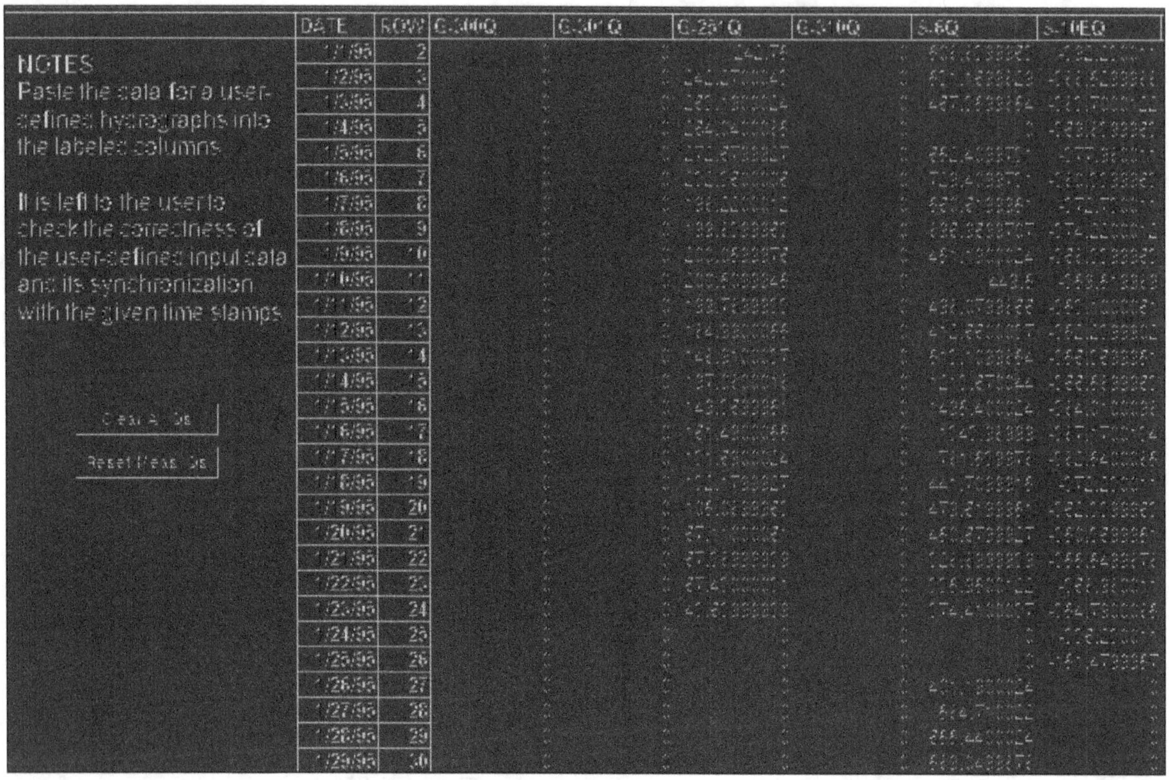

Figure 2–11. Example of "UserDefQs" worksheet showing user-defined control structure flows.

3.7 "Inputs Graphs," "GH Graphs," "SC Graphs," and "TP Graphs" Worksheets

LOXANN provides streaming numerical and graphical trends for input parameters on the "Inputs Graphs" worksheet and as output GH, SC, and TP predictions on the "GH Graphs," "SC Graphs," and "TP Graphs" worksheets, respectively (fig. 2–12). The trend graphs show 90-day moving windows that update automatically as the time step is changed. The "Graphs ON" check box on each worksheet must be checked for its graphs to be active. These worksheets also provide a subset of the simulation controls that are found on the "Controls" worksheet so that the user can observe the behaviors of specific parameters of interest during simulation or manual stepping using the "Step>>" button. A summary of each of these worksheets follows.

- "Inputs Graphs"
  - current values of:
    - by control structure—user input option (Option), and measured (Qm) and user-set (Qu) flows
    - by GH site—measured GH (GHm), GH predicted with user-set flows (GHu), and their difference dGH(u-m)
  - 90-day trend graphs of:
    - RAIN+ET (rainfall and evapotranspiration) and measured and user-set control structure summed flows (TOTQm and TOTQu)
    - by control structure—measured and user-set flows differentiated by "m" and "u" suffixes
- "GH Graphs"
  - current values of:
    - under headings of A3, A10, A30, A90, A210, and A330—the 3, 10, 30, 90, 210, and 330-day MWAs of summed RAIN+ET and TOTQm and TOTQu
    - by GH site—GHm, GHu, and dGH(u-m)
  - 90-day trend graphs of:
    - GHm and GHu on one graph
    - by GH site—GHm, predicted GH using input measured control structure flows (GHpm), predicted GH using input user-set control structure flows (GHpu), and the predicted ε_{GH} calculated by the SIANN using input measured control structure flows (GH-ERRpm)
- "SC Graphs"
  - current values of:
    - under headings of A3, A10, A30, A90, A210, and A330—the 3, 10, 30, 90, 210, and 330-day MWAs of summed RAIN+ET and TOTQm and TOTQu
    - measured SC (SCm), SC predicted with measured flows (SCpm), and SC predicted with user-set flows (SCpu)
  - 90-day trend graphs by site of SCm, SCpm, and SCpu
- "TP Graphs"
  - current values of:
    - under headings of A3, A10, A30, A90, A210, and A330—the 3, 10, 30, 90, 210, and 330-day MWAs of summed RAIN+ET and TOTQm and TOTQu
    - measured TP (TPm), TP predicted with measured flows (TPpm), and TP predicted with user-set flows (TPpu)
  - 90-day trend graphs by site of TPm, TPpm, and TPpu

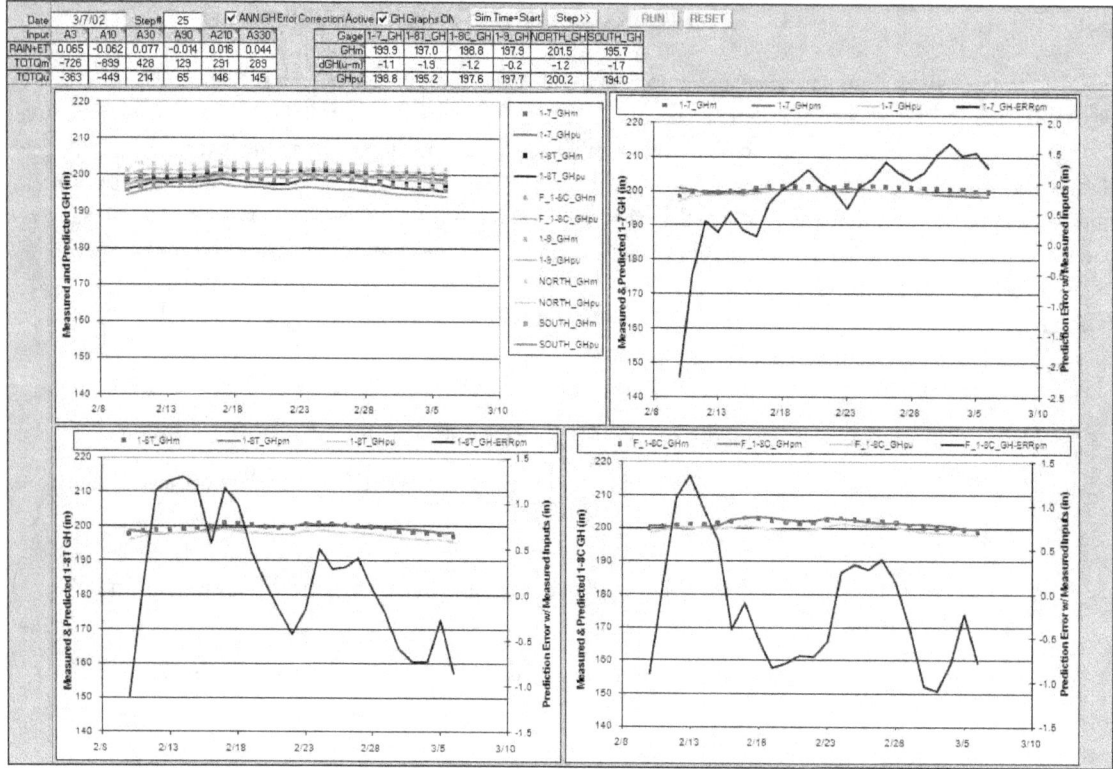

Figure 2–12.   Example of "GH Graphs" worksheet showing simulation controls and streaming graphics.

3.8. "3DVis" Worksheet

LOXANN's "3DVis" worksheet provides 3D graphical displays of the spatial and temporal variability of GH, SC, and TP in portions of the Refuge. The appropriate "3D ON" check boxes must be checked for the displays to operate. The SC and (or) TP models must be active and have been run under simulation for enough time steps for them to generate predictions. "3DVis" provides a subset of the simulation controls that are found on the "Controls" worksheet so that the user can observe the behaviors of specific parameters of interest during simulation or manual stepping using the "Step>>" button. The 3D displays will update for each time step and appear as animations when the models are run under simulation.

At the top of the "GH Graphs" worksheet under the headings of A3, A10, A30, A90, A210, and A330, the current values of 3, 10, 30, 90, 210, and 330-day MWAs of summed RAIN+ET and TOTQm and TOTQu are shown. The topmost graph is a bar chart showing GHm and GHpu at each GH site for the current time step (fig. 2–13). As shown in figures 2–14 to A–16, pairs of 3D graphs are shown for GHm and GHpu, SCpm and SCpu, and TPpm and TPpu, respectively. To orient the user as to the portion of the Refuge being displayed, maps showing the Refuge and location of the gages or sampling sites are displayed to the left of the 3D graphs.

Figure 2–13.   Bar graph on "'3DVis" worksheet showing GHm and GHpu at each GH site.

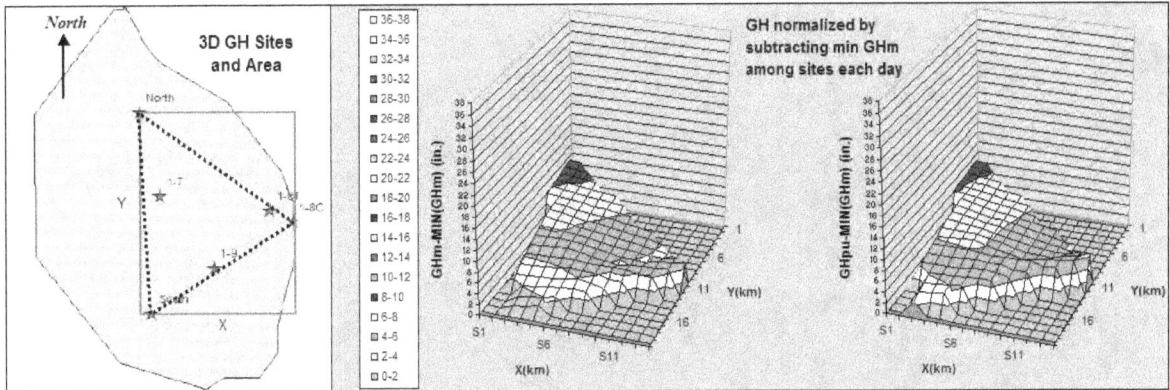

Figure 2–14. Three-dimensional displays of GHm (left) and GHpu (right). Values in cells not having monitoring sites for which predictions are made are calculated by linear interpolation.

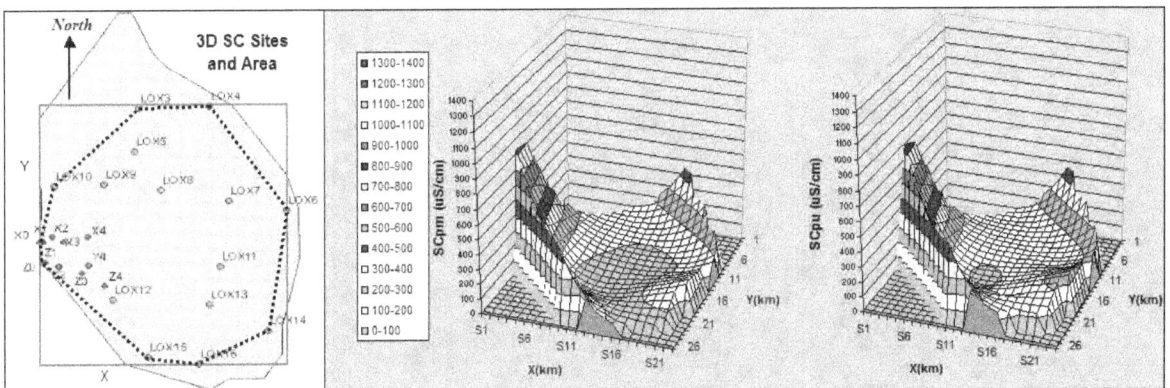

Figure 2–15. Three-dimensional displays of SCpm (left) and SCpu (right). Values in all cells are calculated by the SC SIANN-based model.

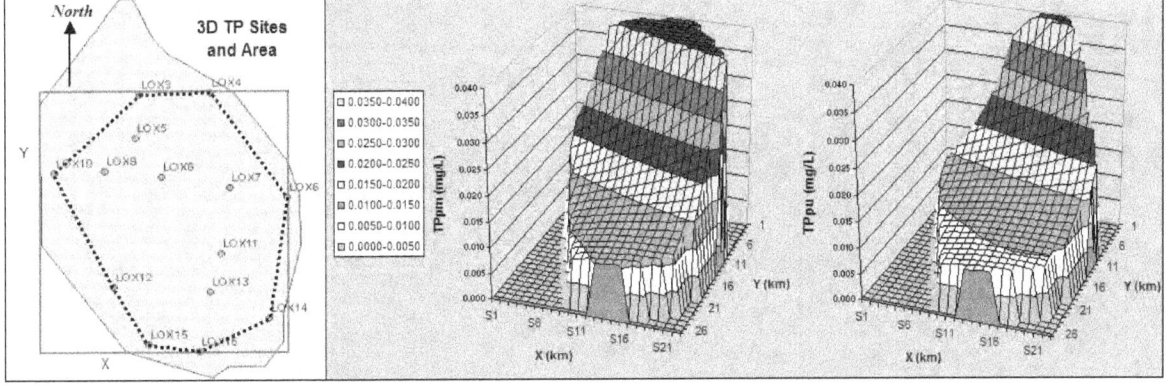

Figure 2–16. Three-dimensional displays of TPpm (left) and TPpu (right). Values in all cells are calculated by the TP SIANN-based model.